PRAISE FOR

It's Your Call
Mastering the Telephones in Your Medical Practice

"To anyone familiar with Woodcock and Keegan's work, it will not come as a surprise that this book should be considered required reading for anyone involved in managing physician office operations, as telephones are the main 'lifeline' to a practice."

WILLIAM PESANELLI, MBA
Practice Administrator
THE UROLOGY CENTER, PC, NEW HAVEN, CT

"As a practice manager you are being asked to do more with less. Patients want to access your services quickly and efficiently and to also feel that personal touch. It's critical that you leverage technology to your advantage to enhance the human interaction. This book gives clear, concise, and practical steps to take control of your key work processes and make the most of your financial, technological, and human resources."

DONNA SCOWDEN
Practice Administrator
PEACHTREE PARK PEDIATRICS, ATLANTA, GA

"This book is an excellent, practical resource guide for any physician office seeking to improve its management of phone calls into the practice. No matter the size of the practice, managing telephones is a challenge in any environment and this book breaks it down into simple and easy to implement best practices."

COURTNEY M. HIGDON, MBA
Director, Enterprise Patient Access Services
UNIVERSITY OF KENTUCKY HEALTHCARE, LEXINGTON, KY

It's Your Call
Mastering the Telephones in Your Medical Practice

Elizabeth W. Woodcock, MBA, FACMPE, CPC
Deborah Walker Keegan, PhD, FACMPE

Medical Group Management Association
104 Inverness Terrace East
Englewood, CO 80112-5306
877.275.6462
mgma.com

Defining Your Profession™

Medical Group Management Association® (MGMA®) publications are intended to provide current and accurate information and are designed to assist readers in becoming more familiar with the subject matter covered. Such publications are distributed with the understanding that MGMA does not render any legal, accounting, or other professional advice that may be construed as specifically applicable to individual situations. No representations or warranties are made concerning the application of legal or other principles discussed by the authors to any specific factual situation, nor is any prediction made concerning how any particular judge, government official, or other person will interpret or apply such principles. Specific factual situations should be discussed with professional advisors.

Production Credits
Publisher/Senior Content Manager: Marilee E. Aust
Editorial and Production: Glacier Publishing Services, Inc.
Cover Design: Deidre Adams

Library of Congress Cataloging-in-Publication Data

Woodcock, Elizabeth W.
  It's your call : mastering the telephones in your medical practice / Elizabeth W. Woodcock, Deborah Walker Keegan.
       p. ; cm.
  Includes bibliographical references.
  Summary: "This book offers tools, techniques, and best practices to help medical practice administrators improve patient access by better managing the practice's telephones. This will optimize provider productivity and efficiency, staff, provider, and patient satisfaction, practice profitability, and patient value"--Provided by publisher.
  ISBN 978-1-56829-430-8
  I. Keegan, Deborah Walker. II. Medical Group Management Association. III. Title.
  [DNLM: 1. Hotlines--organization & administration. 2. Practice Management, Medical--organization & administration. 3. Efficiency, Organizational. 4. Personnel Management--methods. 5. Telephone--standards. W 80]
  LC classification not assigned
  362.2'04251--dc23
                                                2012036434

Item #8596

ISBN: 978-1-56829-430-8

Copyright © 2013 Elizabeth W. Woodcock, MBA, FACMPE, CPC, Deborah Walker Keegan, PhD, FACMPE, and MGMA-ACMPE.

All rights reserved. No part of this publication may be reproduced, stored in a retrieval system, or transmitted, in any form or by any means, electronic, mechanical, photocopying, recording, or otherwise, without the prior written permission of the copyright owner.

CPT codes copyright 2013 American Medical Association. All Rights Reserved. CPT is a trademark of the AMA. No fee schedules, basic units, relative values, or related listings are included in CPT. The AMA assumes no liability for the data contained herein. Applicable FARS/DFARS restrictions apply to government use.

Printed in the United States of America
10 9 8 7 6 5 4 3 2 1

Contents

Acknowledgments — v
Foreword — vii
About the Authors — xi

CHAPTER 1   **Overview** — 1
    Telephones and Patient Access — 2
    Telephones and Quality — 3
    Mixed-Channel Communication — 3

CHAPTER 2   **How to Measure Your Telephones** — 5
    Inbound Calls — 7
    Reasons for Inbound Calls — 11
    Outbound Calls — 14
    Additional Call Volume Data — 15
    Telephone Quality and Service Expectations — 16
    Customer Feedback — 24
    Summary — 32

CHAPTER 3   **How to Manage Your Telephones** — 33
    Process Redesign — 34
    Telephone Action Plan — 35
    Telephone Management – By Call Type — 35
    Hours of Operation — 63
    Getting the Basics Down – Who's on Deck? — 64
    Converting Inbound Calls to Outbound Calls — 64
    Reducing Inbound Calls — 66
    Summary — 71

CHAPTER 4   **How to Staff Your Telephones** — 73
    Recruiting Telephone Staff — 73
    Creating a Telephone Staffing Model — 78
    Staging the Telephones — 85
    Staff Education — 86
    Staff Resources — 88

	Staff Performance Management	89
	Summary	90
CHAPTER 5	**Telephone Tools**	93
	Telephone Scripts	94
	Staff Knowledge	101
	Nonverbal Communication Tools	102
	Customer Service Tools	105
	Message-Taking Tools	108
	Callbacks	114
	Summary	123
CHAPTER 6	**Telephone Systems**	125
	Voicemail	126
	Automatic Call Distributor	134
	System Selection	138
	Telephony Applications	144
	Other Considerations	144
	Summary	146
CHAPTER 7	**Call Centers**	147
	What Is a Call Center?	147
	Key Decision Steps in Call Center Development	150
	Staffing a Call Center	154
	Workforce Efficiency	160
	Call Center Design	173
	Summary	178

Concluding Remarks   179
Appendix: Telephone Best Practices   181

Acknowledgments

We thank our families for their support during the writing of this book. This book is dedicated to the practice administrators, physicians, providers, and staff members who are committed to performance improvements related to telephone operations. We are in awe of their tireless efforts to change this key access point for patient and referring physician communications for the better.

We also recognize Brent Bizwell, Director of Operations at The Emory Clinic, for his contributions to Chapter 7 and our colleague Roberta Parillo for sharing lessons learned in call center development.

Foreword

Someone recently recommended Dr. Jones to me. I called her medical practice to make an appointment and the telephone was answered by an automated attendant. I'm already grinding my teeth when the voice says, "You've reached CSIM&P...." I hung up and checked the number for Dr. Jones and tried again, only to get the same message. After some thought, I realized those were the initials of the name of Dr. Jones' medical practice.

Then the irritating recorded voice tells me, "Listen carefully because our menu has changed." Now I am really worried – maybe CSIM&P is a restaurant?

The recorded voice then announces, "If you are a doctor or hospital, press '1.'" It is clear from the get-go who comes first in Dr. Jones' practice – and it's certainly not me, the patient.

The message proceeded to relate that if I needed to speak to someone in the billing office, I should hang up and dial 555.555.5555, which turns out to be a long distance number. Finally, after several other options were recited, I was told to press "7" to make an appointment with Dr. Jones (each physician in the practice had a separate number to press for an appointment). Another voice came on and said, "Hi. This is Cindy, Dr. Jones' nurse. We're busy assisting other patients. Leave your complete name, telephone number, date of birth, the last four digits of your Social Security number, a detailed message, and the name and number of your pharmacy. We'll call you back at the end of the day. If this message is received after 3:30 p.m., we will call you in the morning unless this is Friday, in which case we will call you on Monday."

I hung up.

This scenario – crazy, but true – is repeated thousands of times every day across America.

Another common outcome when calling medical practices is to find that most do not start answering their telephones until 9 a.m., turn the telephones off from 12 p.m. to 1 p.m., and turn calls over to an evening answering service as early as 4 p.m. When I ask about this policy, I'm told it's because the staff is so busy taking care of paperwork and they must eat. What other customer-oriented business functions this way?

Medical practices have some of the poorest techniques for handling telephone calls of any industry. As we know, people tend to judge quality based on those things they can understand and evaluate. Patients know when they are mistreated by a poorly designed telephone-answering regimen; they naturally conclude that the practice is not high quality.

It's not just about customer service. In fact, we know that the quality of care suffers if patients cannot easily contact their physicians. As a result of the communications barriers we've erected between patients and physicians, patients:

- Do not make timely appointments;
- Neglect to report important information to their physicians;
- Are hesitant to ask questions about information when they are unsure; and
- Avoid calling for medication renewals.

The lack of communication between the patient and the physician can produce catastrophic outcomes – both to the patient's health and the practice's revenue.

We can and need to do better. Please take to heart the lessons in this book. Someone's life may depend on it.

>Thomas H. Stearns, FACMPE
>VP, Medical Practice Services
>State Volunteer Mutual Insurance Company
>Brentwood, Tennessee

About the Authors

Elizabeth W. Woodcock, MBA, FACMPE, CPC, has visited countless medical practices in search of improving practice operations. Educated at Duke University (BA) and the Wharton School of Business (MBA), Elizabeth has traveled the country as an industry researcher, operations consultant, and expert presenter. As a principal of Woodcock & Associates, Inc., and Woodcock & Walker Consulting, Elizabeth has focused on medical practice operations throughout her career. She has served as the director of knowledge management for Physician Practice, Inc., a consultant with the Medical Group Management Association® (MGMA®) Health Care Consulting Group, group practice services administrator at the University of Virginia Health Services Foundation, and a senior associate at the Health Care Advisory Board.

Elizabeth is a Fellow in the American College of Medical Practice Executives (ACMPE). In addition to co-authoring *Operating Policies and Procedures Manual for Medical Practices* (four editions) and *The Physician Billing Process* (two editions), Elizabeth is the author of *Mastering Patient Flow* (three editions), *Front Office Success*, and *PCMH Policies and Procedures Guidebook*. A frequent contributor to national healthcare publications and a sought-after keynote speaker at national forums, she currently resides in Atlanta, Ga., with her husband and three children.

Deborah Walker Keegan, PhD, FACMPE, is a nationally recognized consultant, keynote speaker, and author. Deborah is known for her dynamic, educational, and high-energy presentation style, and her seminars and books are rich with "real-life" case material to enhance learning. They are packed full of tools and techniques that are relevant for today's healthcare environment.

Deborah is President of Medical Practice Dimensions, Inc., and a principal of Woodcock & Walker Consulting. She has co-authored *Rightsizing: Appropriate Staffing for Your Medical Practice*, *The Physician Billing Process* (two editions), *Physician Compensation Plans: State-of-the-Art Strategies*, and is the author of *Innovative Staffing for the Medical Practice*. Deborah earned her PhD from the Peter F. Drucker Graduate School of Management, her MBA from the Anderson Graduate School of Management at UCLA, and she is a Fellow of the American College of Medical Practice Executives. With rich experience in consulting, education, and industry research, Dr. Keegan brings knowledge, expertise, and solutions to healthcare organizations.

To contact Elizabeth Woodcock or Deborah Walker Keegan, please visit www.elizabethwoodcock.com or www.deborahwalkerkeegan.com.

[CHAPTER 1]

Overview

The telephones ring off the hook in most medical practices. They have long been a source of frustration for practices and patients alike. Because the telephone requires synchronous communication – you and the patient must be on the line at the same time – it is inherently inefficient. Yet the telephone is the most frequently used means of communication for patients to access a medical practice. With high volume – and high expectations – the telephone is an area of the practice that is ripe for opportunity.

This book gives you the tools you need to take charge of your telephones so you can:

- Optimize patient access;
- Measure your telephones to understand their current performance;
- Improve the management of each type of call you receive in your practice;
- Staff your telephones to ensure that you have the right number and skill mix of staff;
- Use telephone scripts and tools for message-taking and callbacks to optimize customer service;
- Select a telephone system and its related components to fully leverage technology;
- Prepare for mixed-channel communication with patients, such as texting, e-mail, and online patient portal; and
- Assess whether you need a consolidated call center, and if so, design and implement one that is right for your practice.

Telephones and Patient Access

The telephones are the main driver of patient access and are the window through which patients first view your practice. Yet only recently have they been recognized for the role they play in helping – or hindering – patient access. Historically, there was little reason to focus on patient–practice communication; patients were not only very accommodating, but physician schedules were so full that medical practices had no need to improve patient access.

Times have changed. Today's medical practices cannot afford to overlook the important role telephones play in the success of a medical practice. Consider this: the telephone is your physicians' main link to the public. Without it, patients don't get scheduled, referrals are not made or received, triage is delayed or doesn't happen, after-hours questions from patients are late or don't get handled, prescriptions don't get renewed, and claims can't be followed up. The telephone also impacts the financial viability of a medical practice; over the telephone, we learn the patient's demographic and insurance information to permit billing for rendered services, obtain required referrals, and determine what payment to collect from the patient at the point of care. Not only do telephones affect all of these processes, but they are also the patient's first impression of your practice. Historically all but ignored, telephones are a core operational process that defines your level of customer service.

The telephone is a critical access point that requires appropriate staffing and management to provide value – high quality at low cost. Indeed, in some medical practices, more care is provided and/or coordinated via the telephone than ever before. Nurse triage and advice, case management, health coaching, patient navigation, and telehealth are expanding to provide patients with new access channels for care. In addition, patient expectations regarding service and turnaround times associated with the telephones are heightened, with patients requesting answers to their questions *now*. Gone are the days of patients telephoning the practice and being transferred directly to voicemail, which is checked only a few times during the day. Your patients expect timely and informed responses each and every time they call your practice.

Telephones and Quality

It is important not to minimize the role telephones play in ensuring high-quality patient care. An overlooked telephone message, a message taken that is incomplete or erroneous, or a lack of due diligence in oral communications with the patient, all may lead to serious complications – and potential malpractice risk. The telephones need to be managed and staffed with the same careful attention as you manage the face-to-face visit with the patient.

Mixed-Channel Communication

As we write this book, the telephone used for voice-to-voice exchange is slowly but surely becoming a legacy system. Increasingly, telephones are being used for text messaging and e-mail exchange. In the future, patients will not be required to use the telephone to access the medical practice to speak with one of your staff members. Newer technologies such as online patient portals and social media are coming to the forefront as a means for patients to contact and connect with their medical practice.

For the foreseeable future, the telephone will continue to remain a critical pipeline for patients, referring physicians, hospitals, nursing homes, pharmacies, and other stakeholders to communicate with the medical practice. At the same time, we need to help patients learn how to access us in new and different ways by implementing mixed-channel communication methods, including e-scheduling, e-visits, text messaging, and online patient portals. As we discuss in this book, these newer, streamlined communication methods represent a win-win for both patients and your medical practice.

We organized this book to make it easy for you to access the key tools you need to improve patient communication and access to your practice:

- Chapter 1: Overview
- Chapter 2: How to Measure Your Telephones
- Chapter 3: How to Manage Your Telephones
- Chapter 4: How to Staff Your Telephones
- Chapter 5: Telephone Tools
- Chapter 6: Telephone Systems
- Chapter 7: Call Centers

We have peppered the book with "Best Practices," highlighted to guide you in optimizing telephone performance. All of the Best Practices have also been grouped together in the appendix for easy reference.

It's your call: Use this book as a blueprint to measure, manage, and staff your telephones for optimal performance. Embrace the tools in this book to improve patient access by expanding to newer technologies, minimizing the need for patients to telephone your practice. This book is a "how to" guide to help you manage your telephones – before they manage you!

[CHAPTER 2]

How to Measure Your Telephones

We often use anecdotal data to measure our telephone needs. For example, patients complain about busy signals or long hold times, and referring physicians voice concerns that they can never get through on the telephone. At the same time, employees spend an inordinate amount of time picking up voicemail, taking messages, or calming patients who have called multiple times without receiving a response. At the extreme, the telephone even plays a central role in malpractice cases: a patient, for example, leaves a message with a concern about her surgical site following a procedure; the message gets picked up late in the day, then misplaced in the shuffle the next morning and does not receive a response. The patient's wound becomes infected and her lower leg must be amputated. Had the patient's call been handled appropriately, this outcome – and the ensuing lawsuit – could have likely been avoided. From a pesky operational issue that always seems broken to a quality-of-care issue that results in a malpractice case, the anecdotes help us see that our telephones are broken, but they do little to assist us in identifying the root cause of the problem and taking appropriate action to resolve telephone problems.

In this chapter, we show you how to convert anecdotes to data by measuring the current performance of your telephone system. This gives you the data needed to evaluate the root cause of telephone problems and guide you in creating an action plan to improve your telephone processes.

In this chapter, you learn to:

➤ Determine inbound telephone call volume;

➤ Measure the reasons for inbound telephone calls;

➤ Monitor telephone quality; and

➤ Create telephone service expectations.

BEST PRACTICE

Measure your key telephone performance measures – both volume and quality – to determine patient access opportunities for your medical practice.

To effectively manage your telephones, you need to achieve the right balance of volume and quality. Let's assume there is no change to your current telephone operations. If call volume increases, quality will typically fall, as your employees are asked to manage a higher volume of work. Similarly, if your expectations for quality are lowered, your practice can manage a higher call volume. Therefore, you need the right balance of volume and quality to optimize telephone patient access to your practice. This chapter commences with a section focused on volume, followed by a detailed discussion of quality metrics.

Before moving ahead with any major modifications in how you manage your telephone system or purchase upgrades to the system's hardware or software, measure your telephones in three areas: (1) call volume, (2) reasons for inbound calls, and (3) quality. The measurements play a dual role: they give you information regarding the performance of the current state of your telephones and they help you measure the impact of changes you make as you improve telephone management in your practice.

BEST PRACTICE

You need to achieve the right balance of volume and quality to optimize telephone management.

Inbound Calls

The first step is to capture the volume of inbound calls received by your medical practice. Determine the following data:

1. Inbound call volume by day of week
2. Inbound call volume by time of day

There are two ways to capture this data – electronically or manually. To capture the inbound call volume electronically, consult with your telephone system vendor to learn what data reports it is able to provide. How to access the system's reporting information may also be outlined in your telephone system's instruction manual. Modern systems should be able to produce reports regarding call volume. You can also invest in reporting software that integrates with your telephone system and monitors all of these important statistics. Also, when buying your next telephone system, consider only those that put performance indicators and reporting capabilities at your fingertips.

If your telephone system does not report the data, do not dismay. You can still obtain information through manual tracking efforts. Provide a tracking sheet, such as that displayed in Exhibit 2.1, to your telephone operators and other staff members assigned to handle inbound patient calls and ask these "call trackers" to capture inbound call volume by day of week and time of day.

BEST PRACTICE

Track the volume of repeat calls to your practice. A high volume of repeat calls is a signal that your practice can improve telephone operations and provide more timely patient access. Identifying and reducing repeat calls translate into higher patient satisfaction and less work for the practice.

· ·

Be sure that your call trackers mark any calls that are repeat calls – that is, the caller has called once (or more) previously without getting resolution to his or her question. To do this, ask call trackers to make a special mark on the log whenever patients indicate that they have already called about the issue. If you are using automated system reports rather than a manual tracking log, you may want to supplement these reports with manual tracking of repeat

[EXHIBIT 2.1] **Inbound call volume – day of week and time of day**

Hour	Monday	Tuesday	Wednesday	Thursday	Friday	TOTAL
8 a.m.–9 a.m.						
9 a.m.–10 a.m.						
10 a.m.–11 a.m.						
11 a.m.–12 p.m.						
12 p.m.–1 p.m.						
1 p.m.–2 p.m.						
2 p.m.–3 p.m.						
3 p.m.–4 p.m.						
4 p.m.–5 p.m.						
TOTAL						

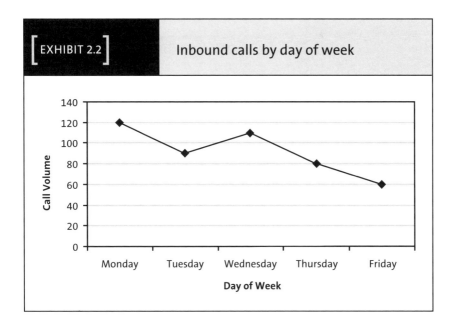

call volume. By capturing data about repeat calls, you learn about changes that may be needed for more timely patient access. Repeat calls are not only frustrating for patients, but also represent unnecessary repeat work and staff inefficiencies.

When you have collected this information, graph the data by day of week, and look for trends. An example of a telephone graph based on inbound call volume by day of week is provided in Exhibit 2.2. As this example demonstrates, this medical practice receives a high call volume on Mondays and Wednesdays, tapering off through the rest of the week. This is a common pattern experienced by many medical practices.

Next, graph the data by time of day to identify trends. A sample graph of inbound telephone calls by time of day is reported in Exhibit 2.3. In this medical practice, we learn that call volume peaks at two times during the day – at 10 a.m. and also at 1 p.m. It is evident from the graph that the telephones are "closed" during the lunch period; as we discuss further in Chapter 3, transferring the

[EXHIBIT 2.3] Inbound calls by time of day

callers to an answering service or routing them to voicemail at lunch or any other time of the day simply batches and delays the work of telephone management in a medical practice.

The graph in Exhibit 2.4 adds the data captured for repeat call volume. You can easily see from the graph that patients are initiating repeat calls with high frequency at the end of the day. This is a signal that this medical practice is not meeting patient expectations for call turnaround times. Patients are waiting throughout the day for a response to their calls and are initiating a second (or third) call to the practice by the day's end.

There may be many reasons for the uptick in repeat calls at the end of the day, but this trend most often indicates a problem related to the processing of work. Calls aren't being returned; patients are calling back to leave another message, to determine why their call isn't being returned, or to simply express their frustration at the lack of communication. The problem may stem from a provider who fails to

[EXHIBIT 2.4] Inbound calls and repeat calls by time of day

take care of any messages during the day, instead batching the messages to address after office hours. It could also be a staffing issue, based on a medical assistant who is trying to room patients and support a physician during a busy clinic session while being responsible for all inbound telephone calls. Whether the basis is work habits or simply not enough people to get the job done, the situation presents an opportunity for performance improvement. Identifying and reducing these repeat calls translates into higher patient satisfaction and less work for the practice.

Reasons for Inbound Calls

Now that you know your inbound call volume by day of week and time of day, the next step is to learn *why* patients are calling your medical practice. This provides the information you need to improve how you manage each type of call.

Although your telephone system may report your inbound call volume, it typically is not able to electronically report the *reasons* for inbound calls. If you have an automatic call distributor (ACD), you may be able to learn the volume of callers who pressed "1" for scheduling, "2" for the nurse, and so forth, but that does not give you the exact reason for the inbound call. For example, a call to the nurse could be a patient seeking test results or a patient who has a question about a medication. To capture the reasons for inbound calls, use a manual tracking form.

Ask all staff members who manage inbound telephone calls to keep a tracking form by day and time for a one-week period. Make sure that the week is generally representative of the call volume your practice experiences. Remind the call trackers each morning and several times throughout the day to keep monitoring the calls. Although you are not looking for statistical perfection, it's important not to underestimate the volume of inbound calls or miss an important category of calls.

To make the job easier, provide a form that allows call trackers to check off the most common reasons for inbound calls. A tracking form that details the reasons for inbound calls is provided in Exhibit 2.5.

It is also important to capture the calls managed by the clinical staff members who have telephone responsibilities. It may take some thought to capture an accurate count of inbound telephone data when you add the clinical staff as call trackers. Contemplate this scenario: your medical practice's telephone operators "screen" incoming calls and then transfer some of them to the nursing staff, but established patients may also call the nurse triage line directly. Consider the flow of work related to inbound calls to ensure that all calls are being captured, but that none are being double counted. Having the detail regarding the reason for the clinical call, however, is so important that it is worth your time to design a call tracking system that results in accurate data. You may also be able to retrospectively review

[EXHIBIT 2.5] Sample inbound call tracking form

Name: _____ Date: _____

Hour	Nurse/Physician	Billing	Referrals	Rx	Test Results	Personal	Appt.	Referring Physician	Other
8 a.m.–9 a.m.									
9 a.m.–10 a.m.									
10 a.m.–11 a.m.									
11 a.m.–12 p.m.									
12 p.m.–1 p.m.									
1 p.m.–2 p.m.									
2 p.m.–3 p.m.									
3 p.m.–4 p.m.									
4 p.m.–5 p.m.									

and abstract the clinical messaging intake forms from your electronic health record (EHR) system to report the reasons for the calls.

After you have captured the reasons for your inbound calls, you have the data needed to manage your telephones, staff your telephones, convert inbound calls to outbound calls, and work to reduce telephone demand – all topics that we discuss in later chapters of this book.

BEST PRACTICE

If the percentages of outbound calls by topic match up with those of inbound calls, look for a better way to manage that type of call by leveraging technology and streamlining communication.

Outbound Calls

Medical practices benefit by monitoring outbound telephone data. Develop a tracking process similar to that which is used for inbound telephone calls. Ask staff to record the volume of outbound calls, ideally by day of week and time of day. It's also helpful to understand the reasons for the calls. If the percentages of outbound calls by topic match up with those of inbound calls, there is likely some room for improvement in managing that particular type of call. For example, a high volume of inbound and outbound calls dealing with test results may indicate that your staff and patients are spending too much time playing telephone tag with each other trying to communicate test results. This finding signals that you should seek ways to leverage technology and streamline communications solutions for test results reporting, which we discuss in Chapter 3.

Additional Call Volume Data

As part of data analysis regarding call volume, calculate two additional measures: (1) call volume by staff member and (2) the ratio of call volume to daily encounters. The call volume by staff member gives you insights regarding the work variability among your staff, which is useful when staffing the telephones (Chapter 4).

By calculating your ratio of inbound calls to encounters, you learn the magnitude of opportunity you may have to improve telephone management. The call volume to daily encounters ratio helps you to recognize the hassle factor associated with your telephones for patients and staff alike.

Although the volume of calls varies by practice, our research has shown that call volume is typically four to five times the number of patient visits per day. So, for example, if your practice sees 100 patients a day, then your call volume likely ranges from 400 to 500 calls per day.

We believe that the call volume should be twice the number of patient visits, a goal achieved by practices that are successful at managing their telephones, reengineering their work processes, and deploying technology to enhance patient communication. If you desire to meet that goal, there are many action steps you can take such as the following:

- Focus on anticipating patients' needs so they do not have to resort to calling you.
- Contact patients before they call you. It's much more efficient for you to take charge of the process of communicating with patients, rather than waiting for them to communicate with you.
- Provide patients with other access channels to obtain information rather than relying on the telephone, such as secure communication through an online patient portal.

We discuss these and other telephone improvement methods in subsequent chapters.

BEST PRACTICE

Call volume is typically four to five times the number of patient visits per day.... We believe that the call volume should be twice the number of patient visits, a goal achieved by practices that are successful at managing their telephones, reengineering their work processes, and deploying technology to enhance patient communication.

You may choose to evaluate additional information regarding call volume, but the measurements displayed in Exhibit 2.6 will offer valuable insight into the challenges you face – and the opportunities available – related to your telephones.

Telephone Quality and Service Expectations

In addition to the volume of inbound telephone calls and the reason for the calls, you also need to examine the *quality* of your telephone management. Exhibit 2.7 summarizes key telephone quality measures. Much of these data are available electronically via your telephone system, such as the time-based measures of abandonment rate, service level, and average speed to answer. Check with your telephone vendor for these options, using this list and the following definitions to guide your data-gathering efforts. Your telephone vendor may also have suggestions for other metrics, particularly for a large call center.

Key quality measurements and their definitions are provided here.

Abandonment rate. Abandonment rate is the percentage of total calls from patients and other callers that were disconnected by the

EXHIBIT 2.6 Telephone call volume performance data

Volume
- Call volume
  -by day of week
  -by time of day
  -by reason for call
- Volume of repeat calls
- Call volume by staff member
- Call volume to daily encounters ratio

EXHIBIT 2.7 Telephone quality performance data

Quality
- Abandonment rate
- Availability
- Average handle time
- Average speed to answer
- Callback rate
- Duration of call
- Hours of telephone operation
- Message quality
- On-hold time
- Script compliance rate
- Service
- Service level
- Staff occupancy
- Trunk blockage

caller prior to speaking with a telephone operator, either because they were not answered, the caller chose to disconnect, or the callers were placed on hold and then elected to disconnect the call. The abandonment rate is measured by comparing the portion of calls that abandon during a defined period of time compared with all calls received (to include those not answered) during that same time period. Practices typically measure both the number of abandoned calls as well as the percentage of calls that abandon. These data are available from a report generated from the telephone company, ACD, or the system's reporting software. The call abandonment rate is a typical measure of telephone performance, but it is not entirely under the telephone operator's control. Although abandoned calls are affected by the average wait time in the queue (which can be controlled by a telephone operator or call center), a multitude of other factors influence this measure, such as caller error in initial call placement, caller time tolerance, and availability of service alternatives. We witness an average abandonment rate of 10 percent among medical practices. We recommend a goal of 3 percent.

Availability. Availability is the percentage of time that staff members are "logged in" to answer calls. The metric can be calculated by dividing the hours the staff members are logged onto the telephone system into total work hours. Availability, which is affected by the amount of time that a staff member is scheduled, as well as the time that he or she takes breaks and conducts other off-the-telephone activities, is an essential indicator to ensure that the expected staffing model is effective. Availability may be measured based on all staff, by site or team, or by individual employee. As we discuss in Chapter 7 on Call Centers, when accounting for standard breaks (including lunch), the most efficient state of a dedicated telephone operator is 85 percent productivity per workday.

Average handle time. The average handle time is the duration of the call plus after-call work. Available from the ACD, the average handle time should be measured and identified by time of day as well as day of week. Although handle times vary based on the type and content of the call, a staff member should typically deliver a consistent handle time within an acceptable range. Having a high average handle time, particularly when employees are all answering the same types of calls, can identify staff with performance improvement opportunities. For example, a telephone operator may take longer than his or her colleague if the operator first handwrites the message and then types the message after the caller has hung up in comparison to colleagues who are able to type the message in "real time." The ability to work in an efficient manner is essential for a telephone operator, and one with a high average handle time as compared to the duration of the call signals the need for intervention. Although there is no standard industry benchmark for average handle time, internally tracking and comparing this measure among your telephone staff give you insights into staff performance.

Average speed to answer. This measure is the amount of time (usually expressed in seconds) the practice takes on average to answer a telephone call. Because the arrival rate of calls can vary dramatically during the day, the average speed to answer is useful to assess and compare during multiple periods of the day that may have markedly different call volume amounts. Typically observed in half-hour increments, the average speed to answer is important to determine the variability of time required to answer the call. This measure helps you recognize the periods of the day where the average speed to answer is, for example, five seconds, and those periods in which the factor averages five minutes. Because the daily average as a whole may be reasonable, practices should observe the average speed to answer in half-hour increments to ensure that the needs of all callers are met throughout the day. If the average speed to answer is high, it's most common that other quality measures (for example, abandonment rate and service level) also reveal poor performance. These measures help to determine staffing changes that may need to be made to meet inbound call demand. Although there is no industry standard related to the speed to answer, we recommend that the average speed to answer the call not exceed 24 seconds, recognizing that the cycle of each ring is six seconds. Thus, the traditional phrase of "answer a call within three rings" could be translated into "answer a call within 18 seconds." Industry studies have revealed that callers typically abandon their calls after five to six rings, so the target you adopt for your medical practice should be below this level.

Callback rate. Two measures relate to the callback rate: first, the turnaround time for responses based on the time the messages or voicemails were left by callers (referred to as "callbacks") and second, the percentage of time that callbacks are being made based on the practice's protocols. Given the importance of callbacks from a clinical, risk management, and service perspective, the data regarding callbacks are important to measure. These callback rates are a function of multiple factors and a reflection of the quality of the external patient flow process for the practice as a whole. For example, the telephone operators must first take and distribute a quality message in a timely manner. Then the responder must act on that message in a timely manner. Callbacks are discussed in detail in Chapter 5. The industry standard is 30 minutes for clinical calls, and we recommend no more than three hours for all other calls. For nonclinical calls, the callback within the three-hour time frame may be a response to confirm receipt of the message, with an *answer* provided to the caller by the end of the day.

Duration of call. Call duration is the amount of time that callers are on the telephone, measured either from the initial recording of the automated attendant or from when the call is taken by a live operator. This measure varies greatly based on the type of call. If duration becomes a significant factor of measurement for a medical practice, the result is that quality is often diminished as staff may be motivated to *shorten* calls. If callers believe that they are being rushed, they will not be satisfied. Moreover, an unintended consequence of placing too great an emphasis on call duration is that it may actually create more inbound call volume as patients call back to clarify their requests. Thus, we recommend that the duration of calls be tracked, particularly for staffing purposes, but this factor should not be used as a primary measurement of performance for telephone staff.

Hours of telephone operation. The hours of telephone operation are the normal hours your telephones are open and available to callers. Historically, the operating hours of the telephone have been limited to coincide with the practice's office hours (for example, 9 a.m. to 12 p.m. or 1 p.m. to 4 p.m.). However, today's medical practices are opening their telephones at least 30 minutes prior to the commencement of office hours and responding to their telephones through 5 p.m., including through the lunch period, with many of today's practices providing 24/7 access to nurse triage. To assess the effectiveness of your hours of telephone operation, measure the total number of inbound calls and the percentage of total calls that arrive outside of operating hours. To obtain information about calls arriving outside of normal operating hours, one can look at the number of voicemails left after hours, rely on hourly call reports generated by local and long-distance telephone providers, and/or review the call volume taken by your telephone answering service.

On-hold time. This measure reflects the amount of time a caller spends on hold during the course of the call. You can also observe the number of times a caller is placed on hold during the course of the conversation with the telephone operator. Like the other metrics, these on-hold data are available from your telephone system, ACD, or your reporting software. Obviously, the goal is to minimize the length of the on-hold time, as well as the number of times a caller is placed on hold. On-hold time is a function of several factors, but most notably the system's performance, staffing levels, and work processes. For example, a high percentage of on-hold time can indicate low staffing levels assigned to the telephone or insufficient knowledge by the telephone operators to respond to patient inquiries. There is no industry standard for on-hold time; however, we recommend that the on-hold time average 30 seconds or less. Many medical practices provide on-hold messaging – practice information or marketing "infomercials" – during the callers' on-hold time to occupy callers and ensure them they are still in the calling queue.

Service level. The measure of service level is the percentage of calls that are answered within a pre-defined wait threshold, typically stated as X percent of calls answered in Y seconds or less. This factor can be reported as a simple, cumulative average over the day; a weighted average based on the actual calls per half-hour increment; or the percentage of half-hours in which the service level is met. This is perhaps the most widely used indicator of quality by call centers, yet there are no industry averages for service level. We recommend a minimum service level goal of 80 percent of calls answered within 30 seconds and a stretch goal of 80 percent of calls answered within 20 seconds.

Staff occupancy. Staff occupancy is the percentage of the logged-in time a staff member is actually busy on a call or performing after-call work. The metric can be calculated by dividing these "active" hours into total work hours. If staff occupancy is too low, staff members likely have idle time; if occupancy is too high, staff may be overworked. Staff occupancy tends to improve with the volume of the telephone operation. With a high volume of calls, there is a greater probability that there is another call to handle as soon as a telephone operator is finished with a call. As the volume of calls grows, increased economies of scale come into effect, translating into higher rates of staff occupancy. Although there is no industry standard, we recommend that staff occupancy exceed 80 percent. It is notable, however, that lower staff occupancy rates may be acceptable, particularly if the practice wishes to maintain a high level of quality. Of course, practices should be prepared to provide additional responsibilities for staff members, such as opening and processing mail, responding to online appointment requests, and so forth, during idle time. The volume of these extra tasks depends on the staff occupancy related to telephone work.

Trunk blockage. Trunk blockage is the percentage of callers who receive busy signals when trying to contact your medical practice. Trunk blockage data can be generated by the practice's ACD, or by its local or long-distance carriers. Although businesses tend to seek a goal of no more than 2 percent of inbound telephone calls blocked, it's not uncommon for practices to set a goal of having enough lines so that incoming calls are never blocked by busy signals. We recommend 0 percent trunk blockage for a medical practice.

BEST PRACTICE

Make sure your callers receive a consistent call-handling experience. Patients will perceive the quality of your medical practice based on their service experience with your telephone staff.

We also recommend that a number of other qualitative data regarding your telephones be routinely tracked and monitored. These include the following factors:

- **Service:** Compliance with expectations regarding high levels of professionalism, courtesy, compassion, and empathy; use of service recovery (discussed later in Chapter 5) when applicable.
- **Script compliance rate:** Adherence to protocols regarding telephone scripts.
- **Message quality:** Compliance with protocols established by the practice regarding the accuracy, timeliness, grammar, and comprehensive nature of a message.

Ensuring that each caller receives a consistent call-handling experience regardless of the employee involved in the telephone communication is essential to a caller's perceived quality of his or her contact with your medical practice. Data regarding adherence to telephone procedures, call scripts, and message quality are not available from your telephone system reports. Instead, these factors are typically assessed through both general observation and a more formal quality-monitoring process (for example, mystery patient telephone surveys such as those discussed later in this chapter).

Exhibit 2.8 displays recommended service standards for telephone-related metrics. Use this as a starting point and develop your own service expectations related to your telephones. In some cases, you may need to determine interim goals, measuring progress to these goals before an "end-state" goal can be achieved. In most medical practices, steady and sure improvement over time is a goal that can be readily achieved.

It is important to recognize, however, that for some medical practices the telephones are so "broken" that dramatic improvement in a short period of time is needed to avoid losing patients through outmigration.

Customer Feedback

To enhance the quality data reported from your telephone system, we recommend the use of patient and referring physician surveys, mystery patient surveys, and patient advisory groups to help you understand the quality of your telephone management. Develop specific questions to request feedback from patients and referring physicians regarding your telephone operations and communication in general. Make sure your patient surveys include questions regarding telephone access and service. For example, include questions such as:

- "Is our staff courteous?"
- "Are they knowledgeable?"
- "Is the waiting time acceptable for calls to be answered?"
- "Can you generally get through on the telephones?"
- "Are you getting an appointment within the time frame you expected?"

These data give you information regarding how your telephone practices are perceived by your patients. These tools will help you move from anecdotal data regarding service quality to specific data allowing you to target areas for improved telephone quality.

[EXHIBIT 2.8] Performance expectations for quality metrics

Measurement	Expectation
Abandonment rate	3 percent or less
Availability	85 percent or more, based on workday unless excused for training or other duties
Average handle time	Set in accordance with practice protocols; monitored by management with a focus on after-call employee efficiency
Average speed to answer	24 seconds or less (maximum of four rings, if manually calculated)
Callback rate	*Clinical:* Within 30 minutes of initial call. *All others:* All calls acknowledged within three hours of receipt, regardless of ability to fully answer the request. Answer by end of day, unless extenuating circumstances. 100 percent of callbacks made, and performed within established time frames.
Duration of call	Set in accordance with practice protocols; monitored by management but not a component of employee performance
Hours of operation	30 minutes before office hours begin until 5 p.m. Open continuously through the lunch period.
Message quality	100 percent
On-hold time	30 seconds or less
Script compliance rate	100 percent
Service	100 percent professionalism, courtesy, compassion, and empathy; use of service recovery
Service level	80 percent within 30 seconds
Staff occupancy	80 percent or more, but depends on size of operation and expected performance quality
Trunk blockage	0 percent

BEST PRACTICE

There is no better way to obtain patient feedback than to ask your patients directly about their experience with your telephone staff. Make it part of your workday to sit down with patients in the reception area and ask probing questions about their perception of your practice.

Mystery patient telephone survey

In addition to conducting a patient satisfaction survey, implement a mystery patient telephone survey. Exhibit 2.9 provides an example of a mystery patient telephone survey. Use this as a starting point for your own survey. If you serve as the mystery patient, do not call from the practice's telephone, your home telephone, or any other telephone number that might be readily recognized by the practice's caller identification (ID) system.

Ask a friend or colleague to call your practice to learn how often he or she gets busy signals, how long he or she waits on hold, what he or she hears while on hold, and his or her impressions of the staff member answering the telephone. The staff members should not be told that the survey is being conducted so that their typical telephone practices can be evaluated.

If possible, have the surveyor attempt to call the practice during each hour block, that is, 7 to 8 a.m., 8 to 9 a.m., and so forth, throughout the day. You may be surprised – and not always pleasantly – by what happens when callers telephone during the lunch hour, immediately after the practice opens in the morning, or just before closing.

> **[EXHIBIT 2.9]** Mystery patient telephone survey

Pick one of these sample questions:

☐ *Can you give me directions to your office?*

☐ *Can you tell me what experience Dr. _____ has?*

☐ *Do you accept _____ insurance?*

☐ *How long would I have to wait to get a physical exam with Dr. _____?*

Practice name: _____ Caller: _____

Call date: _____ Call time: _____

Overall impression:
☐ Exceeds standards   ☐ Meets standards   ☐ Does not meet standards

Was the telephone number easy to find on the practice's Website?
☐ Yes   ☐ No   ☐ Not applicable

Number of rings: ☐ 1   ☐ 2   ☐ 3   ☐ 4 or More

Courtesy of the person answering telephone:
☐ Very pleasant   ☐ Pleasant   ☐ Rude or hurried

Did the person answering the telephone give you his or her name?
☐ Gave name clearly   ☐ Gave name rapidly or mumbled   ☐ Did not give name

Did the person answering the telephone give you the practice's name?
☐ Gave name clearly   ☐ Gave name rapidly or mumbled   ☐ Did not give name

Were you put on hold?   ☐ Never put on hold
☐ Briefly put on hold after being asked if OK   ☐ Put on hold without being asked

If you were put on hold, how long did you wait?
☐ Less than 30 seconds   ☐ 30 to 90 seconds   ☐ More than 90 seconds

If you were put on hold, did the staff member communicate with you about your estimated wait time?   ☐ Yes   ☐ No   ☐ Not applicable

Level of knowledge of the person answering telephone:
   ☐ Extremely knowledgeable: gave complete, correct information immediately
   ☐ Knowledgeable: gave correct information
   ☐ Gave incorrect information

Was a message taken for someone to call you back?
   ☐ Message not taken: call handled by first person
   ☐ Message taken appropriately: received callback in specified time
   ☐ Message taken inappropriately: call not returned in specified time

(continues)

> [**EXHIBIT 2.9**] **Mystery patient telephone survey (continued)**

Were you transferred to another individual who ultimately answered your question?
☐ Not transferred: call handled by first person
☐ Transferred once to correct person with appropriate explanation
☐ Transferred more than once, transferred to wrong person, or transferred without appropriate explanation

Courtesy of the person answering question:
☐ Very pleasant ☐ Pleasant ☐ Rude or hurried

Did the person answering the question give his or her name?
☐ Gave name clearly ☐ Gave name rapidly or mumbled ☐ Did not give name

Were you put on hold by the person who answered the question?
☐ Never put on hold
☐ Briefly put on hold after being asked if OK
☐ Put on hold without being asked

If you were put on hold by this person, how long did you wait?
☐ Less than 30 seconds ☐ 30 to 90 seconds ☐ More than 90 seconds

Knowledge of the person answering the question:
☐ Extremely knowledgeable: gave complete, correct information immediately
☐ Knowledgeable: gave correct information
☐ Gave incorrect information

Level of concern of the person answering the question:
☐ Demonstrated high level of genuine interest in caller
☐ Demonstrated interest in caller
☐ Demonstrated little or no interest in caller

Did the staff member ask if there was anything else he or she could help you with?
☐ Yes ☐ No ☐ Not applicable

Comments to support ratings exceeding or not meeting standards:

_____
_____
_____
_____
_____
_____

BEST PRACTICE

Use a mystery patient telephone survey to learn whether telephone management is optimized for your practice.

Follow these steps to get the most out of your mystery patient survey.

1. **Identify your goals.** Before you start, identify the key information you want to learn from the survey. For example: Is our staff courteous? Are they knowledgeable? What is the waiting time for calls to be answered? Must patients repeat their information or question(s) during the call?

2. **Prepare the survey.** Use the "Mystery Patient Telephone Survey" (see Exhibit 2.9) as a starting point to develop your own mystery patient survey. Although having a mystery patient call your practice one time is a start, it's best to have a sample from which to draw. Conduct the mystery patient telephone surveys over a period of at least one month, with a minimum of 30 calls accomplished.

3. **Find the mystery patient(s).** Depending on the purpose of your investigation, find a patient volunteer, ask a family member or colleague to help, or hire a consultant. Unless you're hiring experienced professionals, set clear expectations and ensure that they have a script to work from when they are placing the calls and when they are queried by your staff to provide follow-up information.

4. **Use a non-identifiable telephone number.** Regardless of who serves as the "mystery patient," establish a telephone with a non-identifiable number for the surveyor to use. Otherwise, your staff may begin to realize that the same number is calling over and over again.

The mystery patient telephone survey will not give you all the answers you need to fully assess the quality of your telephones, but it will provide more credibility to anecdotal information you hear from patients.

Combine the results of the mystery survey with reports produced by your telephone system and with other observations you receive related to your telephones to give a clearer picture of the strengths and weaknesses of your current telephone processes. For example, if the mystery survey reports more than three rings before the call is picked up, evaluate telephone system reports regarding the average speed to answer in order to determine if there is congruity between the two data elements. As another example, if the mystery patient survey reports poor service by a particular staff member, evaluate the time that the staff member is spending on the telephone during a call to see if that signals a hurried approach with the patient.

Patient advisory group
In addition to survey tools, practices are seeking feedback from a representative cohort of patients. Identify a small but interested group of patients from your active population and ask them to meet at your practice once per quarter. This patient advisory group (PAG) can not only give you valuable feedback about your telephone service, but also about other general aspects of your practice. A patient satisfaction survey typically gives you a "score" related to your telephones, such as a score of "4" on a Likert scale ranging from 1 to 5, but a PAG offers you real "stories" regarding your telephones to help you translate the data to usable information so you can take improvement action. Consider adding others to the PAG, such as a human resources director from a local employer; an office manager from a referring physician; a parent, guardian, or family member of a patient with special needs; or another individual who is not a patient but may hear a lot of feedback about your practice. Prepare questions to ask. Listen carefully to the answers and comments, and take a lot

of notes. In addition to providing invaluable feedback, a PAG signals to the community that you are trying to improve, which can make a positive impression. Particularly for telephone staff members who do not have face-to-face interactions with patients, consider inviting members of the PAG to come speak with staff members regarding their experiences with your practice. This "real-life" feedback makes a significant impression on staff.

BEST PRACTICE

> Don't always rely on your own impressions; let the voice of the customer speak loud and clear.

When asked to provide feedback, mystery patients – or your own patients and families – can be wonderful resources to your practice as you seek to improve telephone service, access, and operations. Don't always rely on your own impressions; let the voice of the customer speak loud and clear.

Now that you have measured the quality of your telephones, determine the expected service you want callers to receive when they contact your medical practice. Then measure the gap between your current state and your expectations. This gap analysis can guide you in your telephone redesign efforts.

BEST PRACTICE

> What are your expectations for the telephones? Compare your current performance with your expectations and perform a gap analysis.

Summary

Measure your inbound call volume and the reasons for telephone calls to your practice. Analyze your current quality in comparison to your expectations. In this era of constrained resources, there will always be a challenge in managing the balance of volume and quality. With careful monitoring, you can achieve the balance that provides the level of service that your patients and referring physicians expect. Armed with this data, it is possible to localize the source of telephone problems – be it system, staff, process, or service – and make improvements. In the next chapter, we use the reasons for inbound telephone calls and share best practice tools to help you manage your telephones for improved results.

[CHAPTER 3]

How to Manage Your Telephones

When you recognize the gap between your performance and expectations, you are in a position to take action to redesign your telephone processes. When call volume is beyond manageable levels or if patients can't maneuver through the telephone system, practices have traditionally resorted to solving the problem by adding more telephone lines, buying new equipment, or hiring more staff. These steps may be necessary, but there are other options that need to be explored. Before adding to your practice's current telephone infrastructure, look for ways to improve call management and reduce telephone demand.

In this chapter, we discuss the key reasons for inbound telephone calls and present methods to:

- Better manage inbound calls based on reason for the call;
- Replace an inbound call with an outbound call; and
- Reduce inbound call demand.

This chapter's recommendations are intended to enrich communication with patients by eliminating the clutter and reducing delays in the channels of communication. By using our recommendations to better manage telephone demand, you can manage calls more efficiently and effectively. Furthermore, in some cases, you can turn the need for an inbound call (one that a patient or other caller initiates) into an outbound call (one that your practice initiates), and, in doing so, take control of your patient flow process. By focusing on changing telephone demand – for example, by reducing the need for patients to call – you may discover just how your practice unintentionally contributes to your current telephone problems with high call volume, long waits, and unhappy patients.

Don't just add more staff or upgrade your telephone system. Redesign your processes to improve telephone service, convert an inbound call to an outbound call, resolve the patient's needs on the first call, and strive to reduce overall inbound call demand.

BEST PRACTICE

Don't just add more staff or upgrade your telephone system. Redesign your processes to improve telephone service, convert an inbound call to an outbound call, resolve the patient's needs on the first call, and strive to reduce overall inbound call demand.

Process Redesign

Distribute the results of your telephone analysis to physicians and staff. Engage them in discussions regarding the reasons for the performance. Although more staff can be hired to answer the telephone (and sometimes, that action is certainly necessary), the key is to focus on the processes that drive the calls. Conduct brainstorming sessions to explore actions to improve the management of telephone calls, as well as to determine methods to better anticipate the needs of patients and referring physicians and reduce telephone demand altogether.

BEST PRACTICE

Engage staff and physicians in reviewing telephone data and developing action plans to redesign key work processes to reduce telephone demand.

Break down each category of inbound calls. Further analysis may show that a physician is telling patients to call back the following day to get their test results when, in fact, those results take more than 24 hours to be returned. Or you may discover that you need to do a better job of promoting the location of your new satellite clinic so that patients don't need to call for directions. Or, perhaps, you learn that you need to instruct patients to call their pharmacy, not the medical practice, for medication renewals.

Telephone Action Plan

Process improvement doesn't just happen by chance. It's important to determine an action plan to improve the management of the telephones. Develop an action plan focused on processes related to the telephones, assign a staff member responsible for each action, and develop an action time line. A sample action plan is provided in Exhibit 3.1. Initiate the plan in a stepwise fashion so that you don't overtax the action plan participants. Importantly, you need to separately evaluate each phase of the plan. To ensure that you are on track for improvement, monitor call volume and quality both before and after implementing changes. If you do not see improvement, change tactics and try something else.

Telephone Management — By Call Type

We dedicate the rest of this chapter to review ideas for you to consider as you work to improve the performance of your telephone procedures. Let's now review key operational processes that drive telephone calls into a medical practice and explore best practices that can be used to better manage this call volume. In some instances, we present methods to replace an inbound call with an outbound call, thereby taking control of the communication process with the patient rather than assuming a more reactive approach. We also share how to reduce inbound call demand altogether by using

[EXHIBIT 3.1] Sample telephone action plan

Goal	Action	Measure	Responsible Party	Time Line
Educate staff about telephone scripts.	Develop common scripts. Conduct educational program with telephone staff.	Mystery patient and patient satisfaction surveys regarding ease of telephone access.	Mary Smith	Weekly staff meetings in January–March. Measure outcome at first quarter surveys.
Reduce inbound calls for test results from 15% of inbound calls to 5% of inbound calls.	Provide patients with a take-home tool. Develop online test results reporting.	Number of inbound calls seeking test results.	Bob Jones – Tool. Cathy Johnson – online patient portal enhancement.	Within 30 days. Within 60 days.
Improve the response to the survey question "courtesy of telephone staff" from 90% satisfactory to 90% exceeds expectations.	Educate staff regarding customer service tools and techniques. Perform mystery patient surveys; provide feedback.	Patient survey results regarding telephone courtesy.	Harry Andrews – On-site education. Required Reading: *Front Office Success* by Elizabeth Woodcock[1]	Within 30 days. Measure at next survey.
Reduce call abandonment rate from 7% to 3%.	Analyze data; assess call volume and quality metrics; evaluate staffing.	Telephone system reports.	Tom Smith	Within 90 days.

other technologies and communication platforms with patients, referring physicians, and other callers.

Scheduling

To illustrate the connection between scheduling and poor telephone processes, let's review a common scenario. The receptionist transfers a patient's call to the scheduler. The scheduler cannot determine if the patient is sick enough to "deserve" one of the practice's precious few open slots for acute appointments. Unable to make a decision, the patient is then transferred to the nurse. After the patient is asked to repeat his or her request for the appointment, the nurse puts the patient on hold to consult with the physician, and, finally, the patient is transferred back to the scheduler. What's the accumulated time for all of these transfers? It can easily take up to 30 minutes. What is the value to the patient? None. The patient just wanted an appointment to see you.

 BEST PRACTICE

> Ask the patient up front: "Do you want to be seen?" Turn nurse triage calls into patient visits.

The healthcare delivery system in our country is in transition. On the one hand, most medical practices continue to receive fee-for-service reimbursement; thus, it is logical to turn telephone calls into encounters that can be billed. Some practices make it a rule to ask patients one of the following questions before the call is transferred to a nurse: "Do you want to be seen?", "Do you want to schedule an appointment?", or "Do you want to come in?" If patients are uncertain, the practice's staff can offer specifics regarding the availability, such as: "We have an appointment available with Dr. Jones this afternoon at 3 o'clock." That way, the practice is proactively turning un-reimbursable triage calls into reimbursable patient visits.

Accommodating patients on the schedule as they call with a desire to be seen is a scheduling method that is referred to as advanced access scheduling. This real-time access cuts down on the work associated with scheduling, as well as managing the burden that arises from deflecting patient demand. Without any triage involved, the patient is simply slotted in for an appointment the same day he or she requests to be seen.

On the other hand, as we transition our medical practices to new payment models to foster enhanced patient access beyond the face-to-face visit, the goal is to provide the best care at the right time in the most appropriate setting. Tying reimbursement to this goal leads us in the direction of providing care to some patients outside of the exam room, via telephone nurse triage; telehealth; and secure, online messaging with the care team. Changing the reimbursement system to emphasize prevention, outcomes, and quality will spark a revolution in telephone management, moving us from a generally passive approach – wait for the patient to call and then manage the call – to a proactive approach involving streamlined access and care outreach. Indeed, your practice can begin by deploying a nurse to act as a health coach or patient navigator for patients, or perhaps just taking the simple step of calling all of your patients who have been discharged from the hospital. Either way, you are positioning your telephones as a vital tool in the delivery and reimbursement systems of the future.

Scheduling templates
Beyond advanced access scheduling and prompting the patient to make an appointment, the scheduling template is often the cause of inefficient telephone processes. Many medical practices have worked hard to extend their scheduling templates 12 months into the future. This permits patients to be given a follow-up visit in one year. When patients exit the practice, they are provided with a written appointment card (or automated appointment slip) similar to that shown

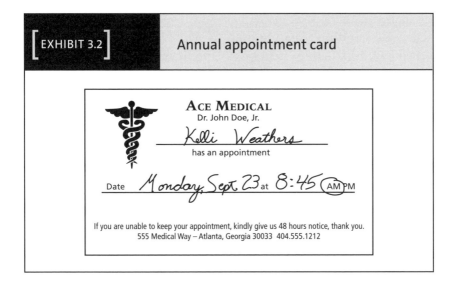

in Exhibit 3.2. But should we rely on a little card to ensure that the patient returns in 365 days? In this world of instantaneous access to information and automated calendar management, it is more than slightly problematic for practices to rely on a little card to ensure that a patient returns in a year.

For a significant number of these annual return visits, moreover, the patient's schedule or the physician's schedule will probably change in the ensuing 12 months – a likelihood that creates more work for scheduling staff who then needs to bump and reschedule the patient, all the while playing telephone tag with the patient.

As we transition to reducing the hurdles associated with scheduling near-term appointments and accept the fact that we live in a world that demands immediacy – for example, same day or next day appointments – many medical practices are limiting their scheduling templates to 150 days or less. In fact, some medical practices schedule only 30 days out. In this fashion, the telephone work associated with changes to the scheduling template is avoided. What also disappears is the blocked patient access caused when a slot – scheduled months earlier – appears to be full but will likely be cancelled by the patient (or perhaps, the physician).

Data you can gather to determine the performance improvement opportunity related to scheduling in advance include:

- Measure the success rate of your patients in keeping the appointments that were scheduled more than 150 days in advance;
- Evaluate the percentage of your patients with appointments who were scheduled 150 days or more in advance who end up rescheduling, canceling, or just not showing up; and
- Count those whom your practice bumps to another time slot because the provider's schedule changes.

If you determine that more than 5 percent of your patients fall into any of these categories, evaluate time periods other than 150 days in advance, such as appointments that are scheduled more than 90 days into the future. Again, determine if more than 5 percent of your patients fall into this new time category.

You now have the data to support changes to your scheduling templates. We are not promoting turning away patients for their annual visit; instead, focus on appointment recall instead of scheduling. For example, determine a new template time line and establish an electronic recall list consistent with provider follow-up protocols. Place patients in your recall list 30 days before their requested appointments. So, if a patient seen in May 2013 needs to be scheduled for their next annual visit, inform the patient that he or she will be notified in April of 2014 via mail, e-mail, or telephone to call (or go online) to schedule their annual return appointment for May 2014. An outbound call to the patient – or a written or online notification – is easier and less costly than managing the chaos of the current scheduling – and rescheduling process.

BEST PRACTICE

Evaluate the percentage of your patients who end up rescheduling, cancelling, or not showing up. Consider changing your scheduling template time line if the percentage is greater than 5 percent.

e-Scheduling

Another way to streamline scheduling – and reduce scheduling calls – is to permit patients to schedule appointments via your online patient portal, chat, e-mail, or cellular-phone-based application ("app"). Regardless of the communication channel, two methods are adopted by medical practices that engage in "e-scheduling": direct and indirect.

With direct scheduling, the patient is able to select a date and time and then slot themselves directly on a scheduling calendar (the schedule is blinded with regard to other patient names). The patient is in essence functioning as a virtual scheduler by directly scheduling an appointment in your system.

Indirect scheduling involves a patient submitting an e-mail, text, chat, or other electronic message to your practice requesting an appointment (perhaps a general request or one for a specific date and time). After receiving the request, a staff member calls the patient to schedule the date and time or the practice responds to the patient in the same method that the patient initiated the request (e-mail, text, chat, or other technology). For example, if the patient sends a text message to the practice, the practice sends an electronic confirmation of the appointment to the patient via text or, if necessary, offers other date and time options to the patient.

Either approach – direct or indirect e-scheduling – reduces inbound scheduling calls to your practice. Importantly, patients are able to schedule appointments with you at their convenience, even if it is after hours. Developing communication channels for patients that reduce reliance on the telephone to schedule an appointment is a win-win for everyone.

Appointment reminders

Many medical practices have leveraged technology, through the use of vendor support, to remind patients of their appointment via an automated outbound call placed to the patient's preferred telephone number. More recently, this technology is being replaced by text messages to the patient's cellular phone, often placed only hours before the appointment time. Patients may even be requested to confirm via text message that they will keep their appointment. Leveraging technology tools to assist in the appointment reminder process reduces the need for staff to place outbound calls – and may lead to lower missed appointment rates for your practice.

Test results

Do your patients have the information they need to know when and how to expect their test results? In many cases, we have found that practices leave patients to guesswork, thus unintentionally encouraging a telephone call. For example, we observed a physician discussing several diagnostic tests she was about to order for her patient. When the patient asked when the results would be available, the physician said, "immediately." With this message in mind, the patient will likely place a call as soon as he completes the tests, perhaps even before they've been interpreted. It's also likely that the patient will continue to call – two or three times a day – until he gets the results or someone intervenes with a more accurate date and time.

Replace this scenario with the following general guidelines that best serve the patient:

- **Be realistic about test results.** Establish patients' expectations before they leave the exam room, and give yourself some wiggle room. If it's usually a 72-hour turnaround time to get a CT interpretation, for example, indicate that you'll communicate with the patient in four days. If the result of the test is abnormal, your practice will likely learn of it before the fourth day and, in turn, contact the patient in a manner and time dictated by the clinical circumstances. In this example, for both normal and abnormal results, you exceed the expectations of your patients if you call earlier than the fourth day. If you call later, however, rest assured that the patient will have already left you a message.
- **Institute formal tools.** Use resources to help patients understand when and how they will receive their test results. Use an EHR after-visit summary or a test-specific card outlining the location of the test (including a map) and the approximate timing and communication of test results. Give this to the patient as a take-home tool, and then verbally confirm the information to the patient. This proactive approach helps the patient – and likely avoids an inbound call to your practice. Be sure to also provide written instructions to the patient regarding the test. A patient who is well informed about an upcoming test doesn't need to call back about directions to the facility or preparatory instructions. Your communication about the test can have a positive – or negative – impact on your telephone process.
- **Follow a standard test-reporting process.** It's simply unacceptable to tell a patient when ordering a test: "If you don't hear from us, everything is just fine." This protocol only generates myriad telephone calls or, even worse, a base of uninformed patients or a problem result that slips through the cracks and is not communicated to the patient. Use one of three notification methods to keep patients informed.
    - **Mail results to patients.** Notify patients as to when to expect their results via the mail. Develop a standard

notification letter, or mail a copy of the actual test results to the patient with a written note from the physician regarding interpretation and any further instructions or follow-up.

- **Obtain voicemail results permission.** For normal test results, obtain permission from the patient to leave a message on his or her voicemail. Exhibit 3.3 offers a sample permission statement.

- **Establish online test results reporting.** Instead of relying on a letter or voicemail message to disseminate test results, provide patients with secure access to their test results via an online patient portal. The value of the portal is that the patient has a written account of the results that can be printed and/or shared with others. Importantly, a portal can display results from the same type of test, trended over time. For example, a patient's cholesterol level trended over time makes a more powerful impact than a data point

---

[EXHIBIT 3.3] **Sample voicemail permission statement**

I authorize PRACTICE NAME, its physicians and employees to leave detailed messages specific to my medical care, including test results, on the telephone number(s) listed below. I understand that when a voicemail message exists, it is no longer covered under the Health Insurance Portability and Accountability Act of 1996 and therefore is not protected from unauthorized access. This authorization is effective _____. I understand that this authorization can be revoked at any time by submitting a written request to PRACTICE NAME. Unless revoked sooner, this authorization to release detailed medical information will expire one (1) year from the effective date listed above. This authorization pertains to voicemail messages only and does not extend to family members and/or other persons that may answer the telephone. This authorization is not required to receive care at PRACTICE NAME. Patients opting not to sign this authorization will receive medical information such as test results personally rather than via a voice messaging system.

Telephone number(s): _____

Patient signature:_____ Date: _____

(This is only a sample. Please consult with an attorney in developing a voicemail permission statement for your practice.)

in time. The patient can see in a visual form whether his or her health measures are improving or regressing and become more engaged in his or her health and wellness. Of course, you must continue to see patients in the office or place a call to those patients with abnormal results or findings that may impact current medications, physical restrictions, and other clinical issues, as medically appropriate.

The key is to *control* the process. While not all patients follow the instructions regarding these tools, even a reduction of 10 percent of the calls from patients trying to track down their results is a significant improvement in reducing the volume of inbound calls.

When realistic expectations are set with the patient – particularly if the alternative is better communication of important information, such as the display of results via a portal – the patient is far less likely to place a telephone call to your practice. By setting realistic expectations with your patients, you then control the communication rather than react episodically throughout the day to inbound call demand.

BEST PRACTICE

The key is to control the process rather than let the process control you.

Prescriptions

Telephone calls regarding prescriptions and medications can overwhelm a practice. Not only are they significant in volume, but the workflow associated with a prescription-related call is also significantly encumbered for many practices. For example, we overheard a triage nurse listening to the prescription renewal line where one of their elderly patients – Ms. Mary Smith – had left a voicemail with the message that she wanted more of her "little orange pills" called in to "her" Walgreens. This initiated a time-consuming process: The nurse had to determine who the patient actually was, the medication that the "little orange pills" represented, the appropriate dosage, and to which of the 23 Walgreens in their city the patient was referring. After that information was retrieved and the physician was consulted, then began the round of telephone tag as the nurse tried to reach the patient.

To reduce inbound calls – and improve the quality of prescription management – consider the following actions:

- **Determine the patient's preferred pharmacy.** Don't wait until the patient calls for a prescription renewal. Along with the patient's name, address, telephone number, and so forth, capture the patient's preferred pharmacy as a basic, essential data element that is always requested and documented at registration. Of course, just as demographic information may change, alterations to the preferred pharmacy should be documented if the patient requests a different pharmacy during a subsequent visit.

- **Leverage the pharmacy.** Replace the automated prescription line with direct patient-to-pharmacy communication. If you have historically accepted prescription calls over the telephone via a dedicated line, voicemail, or staff member, establish a new policy in writing directing patients to their pharmacy instead of the practice. On your automated prescription line, place a message that explains the new process and assures patients that calling the pharmacy results in timely, accurate prescription management. Furthermore, include a time line advising patients when to expect the completion of their renewal requests. If the pharmacy is sending text reminders to patients or otherwise communicating with patients when their prescription is ready, notify your patients regarding the pharmacy's communication process.

- **Develop an electronic interface with the pharmacy.** Request the pharmacists to securely, electronically transmit or fax the request for renewals to your medical practice. The advantages of electronic communication are that neither party has to wait on hold, and both parties have documentation for the patient's record.

➤ **Create an online prescription renewal process.** Permit patients to request a prescription renewal via your online patient portal, with the prescription then processed by your practice and electronically submitted to the pharmacy. The pharmacy then notifies the patient when the prescription is available.

➤ **Educate staff to differentiate between calls for prescription renewal and medication questions.** We often see messages taken for nursing staff or physicians that state "patient has questions regarding medication" when the patient is only seeking a prescription renewal. Of course, patients should be appropriately routed to the physician or nurse if they have a question about the medication itself; however, telephone staff should be asking sufficient information to learn the difference between these types of calls.

➤ **Evaluate your prescription writing protocols.** Call volume for prescription renewals varies by specialty and may fluctuate by time of year and day of week. Some practices, such as residency clinics, which typically write prescriptions for a shorter cycle, may have a much higher volume of telephone calls because patients run out of medications more quickly. If patients don't have a subsequent appointment, the only method of continuing their medication is to call and request a renewal. This process may impact the ability of some patients to take their prescribed medications, as they either forget or elect not to call when they run out. Of course, the standard of care and the needs of your patients should guide telephone operations, but it's an opportune time to evaluate your prescription writing protocols, particularly for maintenance medications. Consider holding a discussion regarding prescriptions, determining whether standard guidelines regarding prescriptions can be established, taking into account a patient's convenience and compliance, as well as the practice's prescription management process.

- **Ask patients to bring their medications to their appointments.** Asking patients to bring in their medications to their appointments helps clinical staff to accurately document the patient's medications, dosages, and termination dates. When patients bring their prescription bottles to the visit, it may add a few minutes to the visit; however, it saves time in the long run. Alternatively, ask the patient to write down their prescriptions (including dosages) and their termination dates and bring this with them to their appointments. A telephone call requesting a prescription renewal is more costly than managing the issue in "real time" at the time of the patient's appointment. Documenting the time and effort that physicians spend in managing the medications – a key driver in choosing the level of the evaluation and management (E/M) code you bill – may be an opportunity for additional revenue. If you adhere to documentation and coding guidelines, these efforts may not only benefit the patient, but also your practice's bottom line.

- **Flag pending renewals during visit preparation.** Steps can also be taken during the clinical preparation for the visit to identify prescriptions that may need to be renewed. The patient's medical record should be reviewed and any pending renewals flagged when the chart is prepared, which typically occurs one to two days prior to the encounter.

- **Ask patients about medications during visits.** The easiest way to prevent inbound calls for prescription renewals is to perform a medical reconciliation at the time of the rooming or intake process of the visit. This helps ensure that the information is gathered and ready for the physician when he or she enters the exam room, and it integrates this work into your patient flow process. Many practices also set the stage for several opportunities to proactively ask patients about their renewals using a multifaceted approach: clinical staff during the patient intake and rooming process, the physician when he or she begins the encounter, and a staff member at checkout. However, rather than verbally prompting the patient multiple times during the visit, an EHR permits each of the physicians and staff who interact with the patient to confirm that the prescription renewal has been addressed.

BEST PRACTICE

Give patients a portable tablet in the reception area for them to document questions for the physician and identify their current medications.

- **Use reminder tools.** A significant number of renewal calls are from patients who have been seen in the last week – they simply forgot to ask you about their renewals while they were in the office, and importantly, your practice did not elicit this information. While patients wait in the reception area, hand them a clipboard or an iPad with a "Questions to Ask My Doctor" and "Medications That I Need to Discuss With My Doctor Today" form to complete. Another way to jog memories is to place a sign in each exam room asking about medications. As noted previously, collecting information about current medications from patients should be incorporated as an expected component of the rooming process.

- **Stage follow-up appointments based on medication renewals.** Time the patient's follow-up appointment *within* the prescription renewal period. For example, let's assume the physician prescribes 30 days' worth of medications and asks the patient to come back in a month for a medication check. If there are no appointments available within 30 days (or the time period ends on a weekend), the patient might be scheduled to return outside of the 30-day window. If the patient is scheduled on the 33rd day, for example, the patient must call the medical practice to ask for a renewal for the three-day lapse. The result is extra work for staff and inconvenience for the patient. Even worse, it may also mean that patients go without necessary medication, potentially negatively impacting their care.

- **Use EHR alerts.** Develop alerts in the EHR system to remind the practice when the patient's medications are about to run out. This way, the practice controls the communication. For example, alerted by the EHR, a staff member can call the patient and state, "Ms. Smith, Dr. Jones would like to see you in the next 30 days; we want to see how you are doing and review your medications." Being proactive avoids the situation where patients are able to obtain telephone-based prescription renewals for prolonged periods of time without being seen by the physician, and arguably results in better care.

- **Integrate the formulary.** Some prescription renewal telephone calls may come from patients who discover that the medication prescribed was not on their insurance company's formulary. Prompted by sticker shock, they call back to seek an alternative medication. Practices with the ability to check the current formulary for each major insurance company with which they participate have decreased inbound telephone calls, streamlined patient flow by reducing interruptions to the physician, and reduced patient frustration.

- **Turn an inbound call to an outbound call.** Place follow-up calls to newly prescribed patients. Use an electronic tickler system to remind clinical staff to call patients soon after their visits if you suspect there could be any concern about the dosage, delivery, side effects, or efficacy of the medication you've just prescribed. Reinforce the habit of making these follow-up contacts with newly prescribed patients by discussing with your clinical team the most common questions you tend to receive.

The advantages of taking charge of the work related to medications stem far beyond reducing the number of inbound telephone calls. Performing the work at the time of the encounter is, of course, best for the patient and can lead to reduced errors related to managing the patient's medications and renewal processes. It is also best for your practice's bottom line, as the physician may be able to code for the work related to the medication by incorporating it into the level of the E/M visit. Performing the work during the encounter, instead of later in the course of a series of telephone calls, may result in a higher E/M level for the visit.

Clinical advice and triage

Patients call the practice to receive clinical advice and triage. Before you add another triage nurse to manage these clinical calls, conduct a detailed review of the reason for medical advice calls. The inbound call data that we obtained in Chapter 2 – How to Measure Your Telephones – provide useful information regarding the reasons for inbound calls. One of the call categories in the tool presented in Chapter 2 is a global category titled "nurse/physician." To capture the questions patients pose related to clinical advice and triage, ask clinical staff to maintain a clinical calls log. A Clinical Calls Log and Instruction Guide are provided in Exhibit 3.4.

Use the Clinical Calls Log to evaluate where calls could be avoided altogether by improving patient education while patients are in the office. Further, scrutinize the calls regarding issues that may have been better handled in the office face-to-face with a clinician. You may be able to develop strategies to avoid many of those types of calls and conserve the staff time spent handling them. As patients seek more "telephone medicine" and only a handful of insurance companies reimburse for it, your practice is stuck with the overhead related to handling those calls. If patients want or need to be seen, schedule them to be seen.

[EXHIBIT 3.4] Clinical Calls Log and Instruction Guide

Patient Name	Date of Call	Date of Last Appointment	Reason for Call
Mary Smith	07/16/13	07/13/13	What medications can she take on the day of her surgery?
Tom Green	07/16/13	07/12/13	His incision site is bleeding and he is not sure what to do.

To use the Clinical Calls Log, follow these steps for best results:

1. Ask everyone in your practice who handles clinical calls to use the Incoming Clinical Calls Log.
2. Record in the log the general purpose of each patient's call, the date of the call, and the date of his or her last appointment.
3. Keep the logs for a few weeks, then review the entries in the "Reason for Call" column. Group the frequently asked questions into basic categories. For example, a surgical practice may be able to group patient questions into:
   - Pre-operative instructions: "Can I take my hypertension medication the day before surgery?"
   - Post-operative wound care: "What do I do if it's been three days since the surgery and the site is still tender?"
   - Logistics: "What time should I be at the hospital?"
   - General questions: "Can I drink alcohol with this medication?"
4. Count the patient questions in each category.
5. Note the time elapsed since the patient's last office appointment and highlight those received within one week of the patient's most recent office encounter.
6. Review the results with the physicians and support staff. Look for patterns. Note which categories have the most questions and which questions are asked most often.
7. Discuss how your practice can proactively educate your patients about the frequently cited categories, and pay particular attention to the questions asked by patients who were just seen in the office.
8. Perform the call logging exercise bi-annually and look for other trends.
9. Seek solutions to reduce call volume – and improve patient care.

BEST PRACTICE

The better educated your patients are, the more efficient your medical practice can operate.

The following strategies will help you implement tools to reduce clinical calls, as well as increase patient awareness.

> Plan for the visit. Establish a protocol for planned care visits: work to anticipate patients' needs by reviewing their records before they present. Identify their needs for recommended preventive care, including that which may have been missed at previous visits or simply based on the timing of the patient's last visit. After they present, proactively provide written information and resources to patients regarding their diagnosis, care, and treatment plan. Providing this support may be incorporated into the role of the nurse or medical assistant; it may also be the responsibility of a dedicated health coach or patient navigator. As clinical staff members become more involved in patient education, patients gain more knowledge about their care. Better educated patients are not just medically compliant, they help your practice to operate more efficiently and enhance your providers' ability to deliver quality medical care.

BEST PRACTICE

Implement "planned care visits" – proactively review patients' records before they present. For patients returning for a follow-up visit, evaluate expected documentation for imaging, lab, and consultant visits to which the patient was referred at the prior visit. Anticipate patients' needs by determining and outlining recommended care to address with the patient during the visit.

- Give patients a take-home tool. Provide patients with a record of their visit, commonly known as an "after-visit summary." These documents can be provided in electronic or paper format to permit a patient to refer to his or her treatment plan.
- Direct patients to your Website and portal for test preparations, pre- and post-operative instructions, and other routine information.
- Ask patients during or at the end of the appointment if they have questions about the visit. Consider introducing a health coach or patient navigator, upon the physician's departure from the exam room, to spend time with the patient regarding questions he or she may have.
- Offer patients a handout with Websites, support groups, or other resources that you recommend. Direct them to online patient resources.
- Proactively address the side effects of medications, procedures, or treatments with patients.
- Develop individualized action plans (based on templates, where appropriate) for each patient regarding his or her treatment and present it to the patient in a notebook that includes a log for the patient to record details about his or her care. In lieu of a physical notebook, consider making the information available to the patient in electronic format via an online patient portal or personal health record.
- Develop a questions-and-answers (Q&A) document. Create a written Q&A form for the top five to ten questions patients have regarding a particular diagnosis, treatment, or procedure. Place the answers to frequently asked questions regarding the diagnoses or services provided most frequently to your patients on your practice's Website or online patient portal, or in a handout to distribute to patients.
- Promote video resources. Develop videos to discuss particular diagnoses, treatments, or procedures to supplement face-to-face conversations and written materials. The video can be

professionally produced; however, making it more personalized to you and your practice has its benefits too. Create a video of yourself discussing an issue, such as post-operative wound care, and duplicate the video in a DVD format to give to patients. Alternatively, post the video on YouTube® and direct your patients to the link. The video can also be linked on your practice's Website. Determine the best option for your practice, and, in addition, provide resources outside of the practice, such as support groups and Websites.

You can't – and don't want to – eliminate of all of the clinical calls, but you can reduce the number of calls with a little effort.

BEST PRACTICE

Videotape yourself communicating instructions to a patient, and post it on YouTube®.

Frequent callers

Some patients have above-average needs for communicating with the practice. These patients – often referred to as "frequent callers" based on the repeated calls they make to the practice – may have chronic or complex illnesses, or perhaps their communication is based on an emotional need. Indeed, many practices assessing their clinical calls conclude that 80 percent of the work is driven by 20 percent of the patients. Instead of being frustrated by frequent callers or abandoning their needs, consider alternative strategies to meet their needs – and yours.

Identify frequent callers, and create and promote an alternative form of communication with the practice rather than resort to the telephone. Alternative forms of communication include secure, encrypted e-mail, texting, or faxing an electronic form via a fax server.

For example, if your physicians round at an assisted living facility, your practice may receive dozens of calls each week from the facility's staff communicating minor issues that are not emergencies but which must be reported. Instead, ask the facility to securely e-mail or fax the nonemergency injury reports to you. Better yet, give your physicians and other clinicians a means to access your EHR system from the facility so they can instantly review, handle, and document the reports while they're at the assisted living facility (or at other practice locations, such as satellite offices). If you maintain patients' records on paper, store those records at the facility and assign a physician to review, handle, and document the calls at the facility. Either method eliminates the administrative demands on the office staff to manage a high volume of inbound calls, message-taking, and follow-up.

Frequent callers may not be particular patients, but rather driven by specific circumstances. For examples, patients who have been discharged by the hospital and/or just returned home from a procedure may exhibit a higher-than-average call rate. Instead of waiting for patients to call, place an outbound call to those patients. Establish a process to ensure that the practice is notified on a daily basis of all patients discharged from the hospital (and perhaps other patients, such as those who presented to the emergency department), with outbound calls placed to each patient. This responsibility may be the function of the telephone nurse(s), or a designated health coach or patient navigator.

High-risk and chronic care patients
Patients with high-risk or chronic medical conditions who need ongoing care typically generate a high call volume. This patient population also tends to represent a significant number of

hospitalizations, emergency department visits, and readmissions. In the new era of healthcare delivery, the practice will be reimbursed based on reducing unnecessary visits at these high-cost facilities. To reduce this inbound call volume – and, more importantly, work to decrease unnecessary hospitalizations, emergency department visits, and readmissions – consider the following actions:

- Provide proactive care coordination and outreach to patients by health coaches and patient navigators.
- Implement planned care visits to ensure that all information about patients is being received, documented, and reviewed, as well as the identification and facilitation of all recommended care.
- Provide tools and resources to assist patients, as well as their family members and caregivers, in self-management.
- Develop an electronic interface with mobile medical devices for patients to notify the practice regarding key patient data, such as weight gain for a patient with congestive heart failure.
- Educate patients on what to do if they are ill or have questions after office hours.
- Institute 24/7 secure, electronic access for patients, such as to a nurse triage unit or physician on call.
- Institute e-visits with chronic care patients to add touch points beyond the face-to-face visit.
- Proactively call patients who have been seen in the emergency department or discharged from the hospital and other facilities within 24 hours. If clinically appropriate, schedule face-to-face appointments.

These actions not only reduce inbound call demand, but they also provide outreach support to patients that is initiated by the practice, rather than the patient. Indeed, these actions migrate the practice into the new era of healthcare delivery – truly managing the care of the patient, instead of simply waiting for the patient to call.

Post-procedure and post-operative patients

For patients who have had a procedure or operation performed, there are many questions that arise. Anticipate those questions and proactively provide answers in writing or video format (see previous section), but also recognize that the event creates anxiety and discomfort for the patient and his or her caregivers. It's not uncommon for practice staff to be irritated or even upset with patients who call about their post-operative care. The pertinent information, in the minds of the practice's employees, was communicated during the office encounter and the patient should have remembered it. The fact is that patients – most people, in fact – retain only a fraction of what you tell them, particularly if you don't reinforce it with the information in writing. Of course, the situation is made only more challenging by the fact that many patients are inherently anxious even if the procedure is routine. It's vital to recognize that the procedure is only routine for your practice, not the patient.

Consider the following action to reduce inbound call demand and anticipate the needs of post-procedure and post-operative patients:

- Focus on the transition of care. Schedule the post-operative visit at the time of scheduling the procedure or surgery. If discharge dates are variable, add the protocol of scheduling the post-operative visit to the patient's discharge process. Proactively communicate with the discharge planner, social worker, care coordinator, or the family to discuss the patient's needs, as opposed to waiting for the patient to call.

- Communicate with patients upon their discharge from the surgery center or hospital. Assign staff to call or securely message patients before and after scheduled procedures or operations to check on their welfare and seek out any questions they may have. Proactively providing the patient with a list of common questions and answers regarding their procedure or surgery may avoid an inbound telephone call to ask routine questions. As we discussed in Chapter 2, analyze the reasons for inbound calls and develop online information and other tools to assist patients in better understanding their care.

- At minimum, place a call to patients within 24 hours following their discharge to evaluate their medical condition, and handle the follow-up appointment during that outbound telephone call. This ensures that every patient who is discharged is sent home with follow-up appointment information in hand or is contacted within a defined period after discharge.

- Supplement verbal instructions with written tools. Provide written instructions on paper or in electronic form, to include video, and review the information with patients before they leave. Or give them a notepad and pen to make notes of your instructions. Patients should be encouraged to write your instructions down on the notepad, or on their smart phones, iPads, or laptop computers. The patient needs to not only "hear" the communication but also internalize and interpret the information through active listening, which reading and note-taking can help accomplish.

- Solicit questions from patients. During or at the end of the appointment, ask patients if they have questions about their visit and the care they are receiving. Too often patients are ushered out hastily after appointments. The few minutes you saved by not prolonging the office encounter are used many times over in handling patients' calls and messages later on. The physician may play this role, and his or her efforts may be supplemented by a health coach or patient navigator assigned this role.

You won't eliminate all patient follow-up telephone calls, nor should that be your goal, as it's important for patients to call if they are having a problem. However, being proactive can help you and your patients.

BEST PRACTICE

If you want patients, as well as their family members and caregivers, to remember verbal instructions and information, give them a notepad and pen with which to write it down; encourage them to make notes on their iPad® or other portable device; or give them the information in writing.

Billing

A significant volume of inbound calls for many medical practices is due to patients calling with billing questions. These calls, which often result in payment, are critical to manage efficiently and effectively. You may have a patient who wants to figure out a way to pay you and just needs clarification regarding his or her bill, but becomes frustrated with your telephone system. You, therefore, are not getting paid. Head off these problems by developing strategies to better manage billing-related telephone calls.

> ➢ Evaluate your billing statements. Take the time to review your billing statements to see if you can prevent some of the calls. Your statement might read, "insurance pending." *You know that means you've sent a claim to the patient's insurance company*, but the patient could be left with the impression that his or her insurance coverage may be in jeopardy. Misinterpreting that to mean that their insurance coverage is "pending," confused patients call to seek clarification. That's not the only source of confusion – complex terms like "contractual adjustment" or basic ones like "applied to deductible" may leave the patient befuddled. If you can't understand your own statements or realize that they could easily be incorrectly interpreted, rest assured that your patients may be having the same problems – and therefore aren't paying. Revising statements for better clarity reduces the number of

information-seeking, noncollection telephone calls to business office staff – and helps you redirect staff time to improving collections.

- Create direct access to your business office. Give your business office a direct telephone number, or route an option in the ACD directly to the business office. Print those numbers on billing statements so patients can call them directly. Set up an e-mail account (billing@yourpracticename.com) or a communication function on your Website or online patient portal to improve access to your business office staff.

- Collect at the point of care. By expanding patient collections at the time of service (for example, collecting patients' out-of-pocket payment responsibility prior to elective procedures provided your contracts permit), you can minimize the volume of statements sent to patients, and respond to patients regarding their questions about their bills while they are in the office rather than via a telephone call.

- Establish online statements to patients and encourage online billing questions – and online bill *payment*. When a billing question is received online, the business office has the opportunity to research and respond to the patient's concern rather than simply take a message and get back to the patient after the account is researched. Inbound billing calls are expensive for your practice; each costs an estimated $4.50 to resolve.[2]

Improving the process related to billing calls can result not only in cost savings, but also the opportunity to improve collections for your practice.

General information

While the areas that we have reviewed certainly constitute a significant portion of your calls, there are myriad other reasons for which patients call, including patients seeking general information regarding your practice. Take action to reduce or eliminate general information calls. Here are some steps to consider for your practice:

1. Provide a comprehensive practice brochure supplemented by a Website. Make sure your brochure and Website include the general information that patients need to access your practice. They should include a detailed description of your practice, including services, hours of operation, financial policies, directions, and so forth. The time that your staff spends on the telephone with new patients who need directions to the practice can be reduced by instructing patients to go to your Website. Include a map with driving and parking directions in the languages that accommodate your patient population. Inaccurate directions produce late patients or cause them to become totally lost and miss their appointments altogether. Be sure to have several people unfamiliar with your location test your driving directions before posting them. And don't forget to include information about public transportation, where applicable.

2. Optimize your social media presence. Increasingly, patients are interacting with social media, such as Facebook and LinkedIn®, to learn valuable information about your medical practice. Establish a professional Facebook fan page and a LinkedIn® page for your practice. Having a social media presence allows you to better serve patients, and they won't need to call you as often.

3. Integrate forms with your Website. Integrate common requests for information from patients, such as medical records requests, with your Website. Also, use your Website to obtain information you need from patients, such as asking patients to download registration forms that need to be completed prior to their visit.

Determine what other needs may be met by proactively providing patients with information. Your patients benefit by making the information readily available, and your practice benefits by reducing inbound calls for general information requests.

Hours of Operation

Regardless of the type of call, being able to respond to calls during the business day is vital to maintain patient access – and your practice's bottom line. Although it was historically acceptable to restrict inbound telephone calls to several hours in the morning and afternoon, practices today recognize the negative impact that these restrictions place on their patients and referring physicians. In addition to the access limitations, transferring callers to an answering service or routing them to voicemail at lunch or any other time of the day simply batches and delays work. Thus, it actually consumes more time to manage telephones in a restricted environment, which is certainly not the intention. Answer your telephones starting a minimum of 30 minutes before your office hours begin, and keep your telephones open at lunch. These time periods are essential to capture the needs of patients and referring physicians, who often need to call you before they begin their workday or during their lunch period.

 BEST PRACTICE

> Answer your telephones starting a minimum of 30 minutes before your office hours begin, and keep your telephones open at lunch.

Getting the Basics Down – Who's on Deck?

Patients call for so many reasons that locating the correct staff member who can manage the call can be a chore. Give each telephone operator a daily list of everyone's responsibilities (unless it's inherent in their job title) and whereabouts. Distribute the list on paper, write it on a white board each morning in a central location in the practice, set it to be the practice's screen saver, and/or reside it on the practice's intranet. Regardless of how it is executed, the few minutes it takes each morning to prepare this "who's on deck?" communication saves precious time in looking for someone to answer a patient's question. It also lessens the caller's time on hold. Similarly, you can extend these protocols to work processes by establishing a knowledge center for your practice. Place scripting tools and practice resources on a searchable intranet or other secure, password-protected Website to ensure that employees have the tools they need at their fingertips to assist callers.

Converting Inbound Calls to Outbound Calls

In our discussion, we have provided examples of turning an inbound call to an outbound call. You might wonder why these recommendations are made: isn't a call just a call regardless of how it is generated? The current focus of telephone management for practices is, most commonly, handling *inbound* calls. Inbound call traffic, on which we've come to rely for most of our patient telephone contacts, is more difficult to handle than outbound traffic. To understand why, consider four facts:

> First, a call requires synchronous communication. In sum, the caller and the person who can respond to the call must be available at the exact same time. Because staff members are not sitting idle waiting for calls to be directed to them, they are most often not readily available – or they are totally unavailable – when an inbound call is received and processed. It's often not possible for a practice to handle an inbound

call immediately, thus initiating the time-consuming – and expensive – process of taking a message, performing the action dictated by the patient's communication, and, finally, attempting to reach the patient again.

➤ Second, because the caller is challenged with gaining access to a particular person or a specific area of the practice, the process involves technology to appropriately route the call (automated attendant, combined with an ACD) and/or a live operator(s). Either way, your practice spends a pretty penny just to handle the call – yet often ends up just taking a message.

➤ Third, inbound calls arrive and cluster during times that also happen to be peak volume times for office encounters. Thus, rarely can resources be matched with the work – the call – without a significant opportunity cost.

➤ Fourth, the inbound calls must typically be processed blindly – when the call is received, staff must ask questions of the caller to pull a paper record or query an electronic record to determine the proper context of the call. Either way, there's a time delay and a cost to understanding the context of the call (and importantly, documenting it). Many practices have integrated EHRs just to decrease the handling time; however, regardless, the person taking the call must take the time to review the information, determine the context, and decide to whom the message must be routed.

When the call can be anticipated or the context determined *before* the patient calls you, the four challenges of the inbound call are significantly diminished. Although it still requires time, an outbound call permits the task to be performed at a lower cost because a message need not be generated or distributed. Furthermore, there is confirmation that the resource at the practice (the person with the requisite knowledge to manage the call) is actually available. Finally, the calls can be made during times when there is a lower workload in the practice.

So, how can an inbound call be replaced with an outbound call? By coordinating the care of your patients. Place an outbound call before and after a procedure or surgery; proactively contact patients immediately after receiving their test results; follow up with patients who just received surprising information; query your registry for patients who have uncontrolled chronic illnesses and provide opportunities to coach them; and recall patients for missed encounters based on your recommended clinical guidelines.

This is not to discount the challenge of reaching the patient, but consider that most patients now carry portable cellular phones. If you don't make any outbound calls, your patients will surely call you. Get started on turning more inbound into outbound calls; it's more efficient and it reduces the need for patients to call your practice.

BEST PRACTICE

Outbound telephone calls are more efficient because you're in control of the work; an inbound call controls you.

Reducing Inbound Calls

In addition to reducing the inbound calls based on the reasons for the calls, there are opportunities that can reduce inbound call volume regardless of the nature of the call. These opportunities include leveraging technology, reducing rework by initiating a "virtual" encounter, discouraging unnecessary inbound calls, and decreasing transfers. Let's take a look at each of these opportunities.

Leverage technology

Evaluate the calls that you are receiving, and determine if there are alternative forms of communication. For example, the offices of referring physicians may be calling to request a consultation. Instead of handling the process over the telephone, create a secure, online request process that prompts the referring physician to provide the information you need to assess the appropriateness of the referral and/or make an appointment for the patient.

As another example, leverage your online patient portal by expanding services and information available to patients online. Clinical and business access options available to patients online are outlined in Exhibit 3.5.

In many cases, patients who interact with your online portal conduct the work that your telephone operators and triage staff have traditionally performed in the past. When patients use the online portal, they are responsible for accurately identifying themselves (no more finding the "right" Mary Smith; the patient has a unique user identification and password); routing their request to the appropriate party by determining their own needs (appointment request, for example); and documenting their own message. Converting inbound

[EXHIBIT 3.5] **Online access options**

Clinical Access	Business Access
• Online scheduling	• History/billing forms
• E-consults/visits	• Health risk assessment
• Telehealth/mobile health	• Survey instruments
• Secure e-mail messaging	• Bill pay
• Test results reporting	• General information
• 3D virtual experience	

telephone calls to secure, electronic messages, routing requests via the online patient portal, and migrating inbound scheduling calls to online e-scheduling leverages technology to minimize inbound telephone calls – and saves your practice both time and money.

Reduce the rework

Some of the activity that occurs on the telephones represents an excellent example of rework – performing and managing the same work over and over again – in a practice. Rework is not only inefficient, it's expensive. Do the work – and do it right the first time. To reduce rework, incorporate the idea of a "virtual" encounter into each physician's schedule. A virtual encounter is essentially a "meeting" with paperwork (note that this concept differs from a virtual visit with a patient such as an e-visit). Embracing this concept, the physician sees patient 1, then patient 2, then patient 3, and then attends to his or her inbox, thereby addressing inboxes – in paper or electronic form – after every third patient. This virtual encounter involves spending a few minutes to review the messages and tasks that have been received since the last virtual encounter. Typically, a formal time is not reserved on the schedule for this work; however, by instituting this approach and formalizing the support role of staff to help make it work, the physician can manage telephone messages (and other tasks) more effectively.

BEST PRACTICE

Do the work and do the work right the first time.

The efficacy of this strategy tends to fall off dramatically if the virtual encounter isn't performed at least once an hour, primarily because the volume of paperwork is too significant to handle in a timely manner. Moreover, the success of this virtual encounter hinges on the physician's support staff to accurately and comprehensively document, as well as prioritize, messages and tasks. (See Chapter 5 for tips about improving message-taking skills.) The physician's inbox should include any outstanding messages that need response, required documentation that needs to be completed, or other pending tasks. When the physicians perform this virtual encounter several times during a clinic session, work is completed throughout the day and very little of it remains at day's end.

If you make the virtual encounter concept part of each physician's day, you reduce the amount of recall and rework time that is now likely part of his or her evening ritual after the office closes. It puts an end to patients calling your practice multiple times due to frustration with your response times. The virtual encounter also increases staff efficiency – employees spend far less time recording, filing, batching, and organizing messages and related paperwork.

BEST PRACTICE

> Make a virtual encounter part of each physician's day to attend to telephone messages, thereby ensuring a quick turnaround time to the caller – and avoiding repeat calls to the medical practice.

Don't just assume that this virtual encounter is solely the physician's responsibility, however. Before a message is incorporated into the physician's inbox, the operator must inquire of the caller: "Is there anything that *I* can do to help you?" If a message is necessary, support staff must be trained to take a comprehensive message, clearly outlining the nature of the communication. Furthermore, the contact information of the caller should be accurate. Most importantly, when the physician offers a response, the clinical support staff must take timely and appropriate action.

BEST PRACTICE

Before a message is taken, the operator should inquire of the caller: "Is there anything that *I* can do to help you?"

If the virtual encounter isn't an option for your practice, consider requesting the nurse to formally "check in" with the physician every few hours to review messages that need to be addressed. Quickly review them with the physician when he or she is between patients. This method of working is certainly acceptable – the key is to *pull in* the work.

By attacking the work before it attacks you, you allow your staff the opportunity to better help your patients – and efficiently and effectively support the physician as he or she sees patients.

Don't encourage unnecessary inbound calls

Examine whether you are encouraging unnecessary telephone calls via your behavior. For example, instructing the patient to "call to let us know how you are doing" may sound customer friendly at the time, but when the patient calls in the midst of a busy Monday morning to inform you that she had a lovely weekend, that instruction does not have its intended effect. On Monday morning, employees answering calls are busy on the telephones and clinical staff members are occupied with patients, thus creating a situation in which the patient's call may not be received in the manner the patient expected. Don't be frustrated with patients who make this seemingly unnecessary call: you asked the patient to call and the patient is only doing what you instructed.

Examine the reasons for inbound telephone calls and determine if you are encouraging unnecessary telephone calls; there may be a better way for patients to obtain information or supply information you need rather than resort to the telephone.

Decrease transfers

Transferring the call throughout the practice is a costly, time-consuming process, and one that can frustrate the patient. Develop internal protocols to limit or collapse the number of telephone transfers that take place between practice staff simply to resolve the telephone call. Route callers to someone who has the knowledge and skill to respond to the caller in a one-call, one-touch fashion. In addition to the staff time, every transfer is wasted time for the patient, and it ties up the line for the next patient. Staff your telephones with employees who can help the patient – or route callers to employees who have the requisite knowledge to respond to the caller with the accurate answer, thereby eliminating the many inefficiencies of playing "pass the caller."

BEST PRACTICE

Staff your telephones with employees who have the requisite knowledge to help the caller, thereby eliminating the inefficiencies associated with "pass the caller."

Summary

Evaluate the reasons for inbound calls to your practice and create an action plan to improve call management. Instead of hiring more telephone operators or adding telephone lines to try and make telephone problems go away, look for ways to redesign your patient flow processes related to the reasons for your inbound telephone calls. Work to transition an inbound telephone call to an outbound telephone call, thereby taking control of the telephone process and ensuring that the caller's request is handled by the most appropriate staff member – the person who has the knowledge required to respond to the caller and get the job done, the first time. Finally, explore the steps you can take to reduce inbound call volume.

Establish your telephone system and the processes around it so that patients can pull the value they seek and get information they need without having to resort to a telephone call. Patients don't want to be mired in a long trek through your telephone system any more than you want to spend all that extra time answering avoidable calls to your practice.

End Notes

1. Elizabeth W. Woodcock, *Front Office Success* (Englewood, Colo.: Medical Group Management Association, 2011). Available at www.mgma.com and www.amazon.com.
2. Deborah Walker Keegan, Elizabeth W. Woodcock, and Sara M. Larch, *The Physician Billing Process: 12 Potholes to Avoid in the Road to Getting Paid* (Englewood, Colo.: Medical Group Management Association, 2009). Available at www.mgma.com and www.amazon.com.

[CHAPTER 4]

How to Staff Your Telephones

It is important to not only hire the right type of staff for the telephones, but also to ensure that you have the right volume and skill mix of staff to effectively manage the telephones in your medical practice. Importantly, the work assignments of telephone staff members and the training and resources provided to them lay the groundwork for telephone success.

In this chapter, we discuss the nuances of staffing your telephones to include:

- Recruiting telephone staff;
- The right type, volume, and skill mix of staff members for the telephones;
- Staff work assignments;
- Staff training and resources; and
- Staff performance management.

Although there are ways to decrease your call volume, there will always be telephone calls to a medical practice – and there must be people to answer them. The key is to ensure that you have the right number of people with the right skill mix to effectively manage your telephones.

Recruiting Telephone Staff

Recognizing the importance of the telephones to medical practice success, it is puzzling to see many medical practices delegate the telephones, the vital lifeline to patient access, to the lowest paid, least trained, and, often, least experienced staff members. In addition to redesigning the "what" and "how" of handling the telephones, be sure to look carefully at *who* you hire (or have hired) to answer the telephones. The employee who answers your telephone represents your patients' first "moment of truth" with your practice, and determines whether patients' questions or concerns are routed to the correct party. This employee, often referred to as a telephone operator, is usually the individual who also schedules an appointment on behalf of the patient. Indeed, the schedule defines the execution of your practice's most precious asset – your providers' time. Investing in this critical position cannot be overlooked.

Telephone operators need knowledge of medical practice operations and must possess customer service skills. Many medical practices are staffing their telephone operations with employees who have clinical training. With clinical knowledge, staff can follow your protocols to ask appropriate follow-up questions that ensure a complete message is taken, as well as determine the type of patient visit and urgency of the visit that is needed.

BEST PRACTICE

Your telephone operator represents the patient's first impression of your practice. Make sure the employee has the knowledge and skills to manage a high volume of calls with quality and compassion.

Pre-employment assessment

Having the right staff starts with *hiring* the right staff. Consideration should be given to including "tests" in the hiring process. (See Exhibit 4.1 for a sample pre-employment questionnaire.) Spelling, grammar, clinical terminology, telephone management, and similar tools to assess the candidate should be considered to improve hiring

> **[EXHIBIT 4.1]** **Pre-employment questionnaire**

1. [Evaluation of candidate's service orientation and effectiveness.] When a patient calls, what would you suggest as the initial greeting?
2. [Evaluation of ability for candidate to take a comprehensive, legible message.] Please take a message based on this information. "Hi, my name is Susie. I'm calling on behalf of my elderly mother. She was seen by one of your doctors early last year and has had some recurring issues in her left knee. She has limited transportation available to her and would like to make an appointment for the morning of November 7th to see Dr. Smith. Is he available and what information can be completed ahead of time?"
3. [Evaluation of grammar skills.] Please review the following message, and identify the mistakes that you see. (Provide the message to the candidate.)

    Judy Jones (DOB 6/23/76) called today with quetions about her medicatin. She developed a rash on her toursoe, and is having trouebl swallowing food. The last doos of medicine she took was yesterday mrning. She kneads to speak with someone twoday. Please call her this even ing at 404.333.111.

4. [Evaluation of ability to multitask.] When taking calls, you are on a headset talking while simultaneously typing messages. A patient calls with a convoluted insurance question that you don't understand. You must both take the message and respond to the patient according to the policies and procedures from the insurance handbook; however, you are not able to locate the answer in the handbook. How do you handle this situation?
5. [Evaluation of ability to cope with change.] Three weeks after you start and having been extensively trained on the telephone system, the practice upgrades to a new telephone system that you find difficult to learn. How do you handle this change?
6. [Evaluation of ability to work under pressure.] Your manager has set a deadline to complete several tasks by the end of your shift. As the deadline approaches, you have just enough time to complete the tasks when you get a call from an irate patient who has been waiting all day to receive a callback from his physician. How do you handle this situation?
7. [Evaluation of ability to handle difficult situations.] You are assisting a patient with an immediate need when two additional calls come in at the same time. How do you handle this situation?
8. [Evaluation of ability to deal with challenges.] A patient calls and is very upset. He becomes more belligerent during the call and begins using profanity directed toward you. How do you respond?
9. [Evaluation of team work.] How would your (former) peers describe you?
10. Which software applications have you used? What products and services have you dealt with? What is the typical call volume you have experienced in a single day?

(continues)

[EXHIBIT 4.1]	Pre-employment questionnaire (continued)

11. What do you like most about being a telephone operator? What do you like the least?
12. If there was one reason that we should select you over the other applicants, what would that be?
13. Why do you want to work for our organization?

selections. When you find the right candidate, request a working interview. Typically a paid half- or full-day, this "interview" – also referred to as a "job shadow" – is a chance for the candidate to understand the job by actually experiencing it, and it allows the practice to assess the candidate outside of a formal job interview.

 BEST PRACTICE

Having the right staff starts with hiring the right staff.

Hiring philosophy

It is rare for a job candidate to have all of the knowledge and skills you require in the role of a telephone operator for a medical practice. The candidates tend to have strong medical practice knowledge and skills – or they have a strong customer service background. With that in mind, determine your philosophy regarding staff hires. Do you want to hire for medical practice knowledge and then educate the new hire to customer service? Or do you want to hire for customer service and then educate the new hire to medical practice knowledge? When it comes to the telephones, many medical practices have elected the second approach – hiring staff with excellent customer service backgrounds and then conducting staff training for medical terminology and medical practice operations.

 BEST PRACTICE

Many medical practices have elected to hire staff with excellent customer service backgrounds and then train for medical terminology and medical practice operations.

As medical practices recognize the importance of the telephones to patient access and overall practice success, more innovative staffing models are being adopted to ensure that all staff members have customer service skills, as well as knowledge of medical practice operations. For example, some medical practices employ "access coordinators" to respond to the telephone, as well as schedule appointments and take messages. Others appoint all staff members as "clinical associates" – super-trained staff who are able to manage telephones, the front office, and back office clinical support. In these situations, a dual focus on customer service skills and medical practice knowledge ensures that employees have the requisite knowledge to manage all customer-service interactions to a high level.[1]

Identifying candidates

Most practices rely on placing a job advertisement in the local media, contracting with a staffing company, or asking existing staff to help identify candidates to aid in the search for a new employee. Besides these traditional hiring methods, practices are finding success with identifying candidates via online sites like Monster.com. LinkedIn® is also an excellent source for posting information about your new position. Don't forget to access social media to evaluate a candidate's fit with your medical practice. Their customer service skills are often highly evident from their Facebook, LinkedIn®, and/or Twitter® accounts or other social media. Don't overlook these newer tools to assess a candidate's appropriateness. Of course, a background check is a necessity for all employees today. Consult with an attorney regarding opportunities to evaluate the backgrounds of your candidates.

BEST PRACTICE

Use social media to identify candidates and to evaluate the candidate's fit with your medical practice.

Creating a Telephone Staffing Model

Forget trying to staff your telephones based on how many physicians each employee serves. The number of employees you need depends on how many telephone calls need to be answered, and the level of service you want to provide. Telephone call volume fluctuates by day and by time of day, hence the requirement to create a flexible staffing model rather than a static model. If a medical practice assigns the same number of staff members to the telephones regardless of call volume, the telephones will likely be either over- or understaffed.

To build the staffing model for telephones, use the data you captured in Chapter 2 – How to Measure Your Telephones. This included: (1) inbound call volume by day of week, (2) inbound call volume by time of day, and (3) inbound call volume by reason for call. The first two measures are useful in determining the number of staff members you need to assign to the telephones in your practice. The third measure – inbound telephone calls by reason for call – helps you determine the skill mix you need for staffing your telephones. For example, a high volume of clinical calls may signal the need to establish a telephone nurse triage unit for your medical practice. As discussed in further detail below, your practice should also account for the desired level of timeliness and quality of the telephone communications when staffing the telephones.

BEST PRACTICE

To determine the number of staff members you need to manage your telephones, use staff workload ranges. Be sure to also account for the desired level of work quality you expect from your telephone staff.

To determine the number of staff members needed to manage inbound telephone calls, we first employ expected staff workload ranges. The staff workload ranges depend on patient population, information systems, level of automation, and work processes your practice has embraced. For example, if your staff members are required to gather and/or deliver more information in each call than peer practices, you will have a longer transaction time and therefore should expect staff to work at the lower end of the productivity range. As another example, if your employees have complex telephone processes, they may need more time than staff members in other medical practices to perform their work, again suggesting the low end of the workload range.

Given these influencing variables, don't just embrace and apply the staff workload ranges. Instead, measure the time it takes your staff to handle each type of telephone call, compute an average transaction time, and apply that transaction time to reach your practice's ideal workload range.

Based on average transaction times, the workload ranges for telephone staff are reported in Exhibit 4.2.

Exhibit 4.3 demonstrates a method to identify the volume of staff needed to manage the telephones, accounting for the variation

[**EXHIBIT 4.2**] **Workload ranges for telephone staff**

The following workload ranges are expected from staff involved in call management, based on average transaction times.*

Practice Operations Task	Workload Range
Telephones with messaging	300 to 500 calls per day
Telephones with routing	1,000 to 1,200 calls per day
Appointment scheduling with mini-registration	75 to 125 calls per day
Appointment scheduling with full registration	50 to 75 calls per day
Nurse triage	65 to 85 calls per day

*The workload range depends on patient population, information system, level of automation, and work processes used at the practice. The workload ranges have been built assuming a seven-hour productive day with one staff member performing this function full time.
Source: Woodcock, Elizabeth W. 2010. *Mastering Patient Flow*. Reprinted with permission from the Medical Group Management Association, 104 Inverness Terrace East, Englewood, Colorado 80112. 877.ASK.MGMA, www.MGMA.com.

in arrival rates of the calls by day of week. This method uses data from the medical practice regarding the inbound calls and the staff workload ranges expected of telephone operators. In this exhibit, the number of scheduling calls and the number of calls that require a message to be taken is reflected for each day of the week (Monday through Friday). The expected staff workload range is then reported for each day based on the type of call – scheduling vs. message-taking. With this data in hand, the practice can simply do the math: Divide the number of calls by the workload that is expected to arrive at the number of staff full-time equivalents (FTEs) needed to manage the telephones.

As demonstrated in Exhibit 4.3, 2.50 staff FTEs are needed to manage scheduling calls on Monday and only .50 FTE is required for Friday.

[EXHIBIT 4.3] Staffing the telephones

	Monday	Tuesday	Wednesday	Thursday	Friday
Scheduling calls	250	200	150	100	50
Staff expectation	*100*	*100*	*100*	*100*	*100*
Required staff FTE	2.50	2.00	1.50	1.00	.50
Message calls	500	400	300	200	100
Staff expectation	*400*	*400*	*400*	*400*	*400*
Required staff FTE	1.25	1.00	.75	.50	.25

Similarly, 1.25 staff FTEs are required to take messages on Monday, reducing to .25 FTE on Friday. This exercise helps to evaluate the volume of staff you have assigned to your telephones to make sure it is linked to the actual work that needs to be performed, recognizing that the work varies by day of week. To refine your staffing analysis, measure and assess data based on hours per day. As discussed below and in Chapter 7, the workload associated with telephones can vary significantly, so staffing strategies that include part-time or temporary staff are commonly used by today's medical practices.

Accounting for quality

Although staffing based on these quantitative data regarding the transactions is important, be sure to consider the level of service you expect to deliver to patients and referring physicians who call. Because the arrival of calls is sporadic, it is essential to develop a staffing plan that accounts for the transactions represented by the calls, as well as the level of service desired by the practice. Use the quality indicators presented in Chapter 2 and the more detailed telephone management strategies outlined in Chapter 3 to refine your staffing model. Because the arrival times of calls varies throughout the day, in general, a practice may need to employ more staff than the workload range data alone would suggest to meet or exceed the desired level of quality. Before overstaffing, however, recognize that other initiatives, to include changing the demand for calls, should be deployed.

Employee downtime

A warning about staffing your telephones: employees who answer the telephones, like all of us, have a tendency to pace their work to match the demands of the moment. Let's look at a case study of this scenario in action to see the impact it has on telephone work in the medical practice.

> ### ▪ CASE STUDY ▪
>
> **Orthopaedic Surgery Associates**
>
> Orthopaedic Surgery Associates (OSA), a busy orthopaedic surgery practice, looked for ways to reduce staff. During its telephone analysis, OSA realized that the volume of incoming telephone calls was much greater on Mondays, then decreased as the week went on. However, on Fridays, even though the call volume was lower, the operators' time on the telephone was higher per call. The operators spent 25 percent more time per call on Fridays because they expanded their efforts to match the demands of the moment.

This is a natural phenomenon, but it's often hidden. Even the manager of OSA thought that the practice needed another operator. Rather than hire another operator, however, consider the following actions:

- ➢ Share this data with your telephone staff so they see their work pace, and trend this over time so they can see their fluctuating call times; and

> Don't let this "Friday pace of practice" lead you to unnecessarily increase overhead; instead staff for the work.

In this case, rather than hiring additional telephone staff for the entire week, OSA hired a part-time staff member to work on Mondays, effectively staffing for the work.

Estimate your staffing needs based on how you have configured your telephone operations and the workload ranges listed in Exhibit 4.2. Don't take the workload ranges at pure face value – if an operator must walk from his or her desk to deliver every message to the nurses' station, for example, then adjust the expected workload range to reflect the additional time for this courier function.

Staff skill mix

Now that you have the volume of telephone staff needed by day (and, upon further refinement, by hour of day), it's time to identify the skill mix you require to successfully staff your telephones. To perform this analysis, use the data you gleaned in Chapter 2 when you measured your telephones related to the reason for inbound call to determine your volume of clinical-related calls and your volume of business-related calls.

Clinical calls require knowledge of medical issues to respond to the patient, which may involve decisions about triage, advice, prescriptions, test results, or other similar clinical issues. Business calls are those that relate to scheduling, general questions, billing, referrals, and other nonclinical issues for the medical practice. Armed with this data, you can work to align your staffing skill mix needs to meet the patient inbound call demand by type of call. Use the workload ranges outlined previously in Exhibit 4.2 to build the number of staff needed to manage the telephones based on type of call – clinical or business – while accounting for the work quality you expect to be delivered. The following case study provides an example of this approach.

> ### ▪ CASE STUDY ▪
>
> **Family Medicine Associates**
>
> Family Medicine Associates (FMA) receives 500 inbound calls per day. Let's further assume that FMA captured the reasons for these calls and learned that half of the calls are for clinical issues and half are for business issues, with half of the business calls involving scheduling and half involving message-taking. FMA uses the staff workload range benchmarks reported in Exhibit 4.2 to build its staffing model.
>
> **Clinical calls:** Inbound clinical calls total 250. Divide 250 by the benchmark of 65 to 85 calls per day for nurse triage to determine that you need 2.94 to 3.85 FTE staff to manage clinical calls.
>
> **Business calls:** Inbound business calls total 250, with 125 for scheduling and 125 for message-taking. Divide 125 by the benchmark of 300 to 500 calls per day for message-taking to determine that your staffing need is .25 to .42 FTEs to manage the message-taking calls. Then divide 125 by the benchmark of 50 to 75 calls per day for scheduling with full registration to determine your staffing need of 1.67 to 2.50 FTEs to manage the scheduling calls. Adding these together, FMA recognizes that it needs 1.92 to 2.92 FTE staff (rounded to 2.00 to 3.00 FTE staff) to meet its current inbound business call demand.

Refine these data based on day of week and time of day to develop the staffing model needed to manage your inbound call demand. Next, consider the level of quality that you expect to deliver, noting that high levels of quality typically require additional staffing rather than relying exclusively on the estimates derived based on volume.

It is also important to review the inbound call volume and abandonment rates in "real time" to redeploy staff as appropriate to manage peak demand. If, for example, a higher volume of calls than typically received is coming into the practice, additional staff may be needed for defined time periods or the practice may need to assign another employee(s) to log into the telephones to assist with management of inbound calls. The goal should be to meet the expected performance standards while still providing quality service to patients, referring physicians, and other callers.

Chapter 7 provides additional discussion about staffing, accounting for volume and quality.

Staging the Telephones

Get the telephones "off stage" to separate the work of the face-to-face visit from that of the telephones. In this manner, front office staff members either arrive and exit patients *or* they are assigned to the telephones, not both. Telephone work should not be performed in front of patients who are arriving to or departing from the practice.

BEST PRACTICE

Get the telephones "off stage," separating the work of the telephones from the face-to-face visit with the patient.

Similarly, clinical staff members either support the visit itself or are assigned telephone responsibilities (and increasingly, virtual medicine responsibilities such as handling secure, electronic messaging with patients). That is, nurses or other clinical staff members are assigned to assist with the patient visit *or* are assigned to work on the telephones, not generally both roles. In this fashion, the employees are fully devoted to their respective work tasks. By concentrating the work, one nurse is able to manage the inbound call demand of three to five providers (depending on inbound call volume), thus centralizing this role within the medical practice or within a medical practice pod or suite of physicians. The alternative would be for each nurse to assume telephone responsibilities throughout the day in addition to their face-to-face time with the provider and patient. Intermixing telephone and face-to-face responsibilities is a sure-fire prescription for less than optimum performance in both areas, particularly given the new and expanded roles for clinical support staff to support accountable care, pay-for-performance, medical home models of care, and value-based purchasing requirements.

Regardless of where the telephone operators are located, provide staff members with cordless headsets so they can be mobile as they talk with callers and to improve ergonomics related to telephone work.

Staff Education

One of the best ways to educate staff to handle telephones is to assign a high-performing staff member to provide on-site training support. Most telephone systems permit additional staff – a high-performing staff member and new hire, in this case – to listen in to calls. After hands-on system training, have the new hire spend up to a week listening, watching, and learning from the high-performing staff member. Then reverse roles with the current staff member observing the new hire as he or she responds to patient inquiries.

Discontinue training at peak call volume periods to permit the current staff members to be fully deployed in their work. During these periods, the new hires may be assigned to review scripting, conduct role playing with the manager, and other similar work that furthers their orientation and training to the job.

If resources allow, assign a staff member to perform quality assurance (QA) audits and training. This involves sampling telephone calls (if recorded), work that stems from telephone calls (for example, registration, scheduling, and message-taking), and other qualitative measures. The QA auditor/trainer may be tasked to work especially with new staff members; however, routine audits of all telephone staff are recommended. (See Chapter 7 for further discussion about quality related to staffing.)

During periods of low call volume, rotate the new telephone staff to the clinical area to observe patient flow. This rotation should be limited to one or two hours at a time, with the staff member assigned to "shadow" a nurse or medical assistant who is handling inbound clinical calls. This exposure enhances the fund of knowledge of telephone operators and improves their decision-making and judgment skills as they respond to patient inquiries.

BEST PRACTICE

During periods of low call volume, rotate new telephone staff to the clinical area to observe patient flow and "shadow" a nurse to improve knowledge and decision-making skills.

Be sure to train a select group of additional employees to manage the telephones so they can work when telephone operators and nurse triage telephone staff are on vacation, out ill, or taking an extended leave. Consider the use of per diem staff who can be called in on short notice to work the telephones during unplanned staff absences.

Develop an education and training program that goes beyond policies and procedures and encompasses more than the knowledge typically gathered during one-on-one operator-to-operator training. For those handling nonclinical calls, this extended training should include some clinical education about common – and not-so-common – reasons for calls, medication questions, and handling urgent issues. Task the manager with leading staff in role-playing exercises, joint meetings with nursing and front office staff regarding call management, and discussions of required reading from articles or other materials. (See Chapter 7 for a discussion regarding the development of a knowledge center to be used for successfully managing scheduling protocols.)

It is essential that you clearly outline, in writing, clinical calls that must be immediately "escalated" because they require clinical judgment. These escalated calls should not trigger a response from the operator (unless he or she has the appropriate clinical training), but rather signal a circumvention of the standard message-taking protocol and an immediate need for someone on the clinical team to handle the call. It is recommended that a nurse coordinator, physician, and medical director, in that order, be assigned the "next-call" responsibility so that escalated calls never go unhandled. Guidance to determine calls that should be escalated, and the methods by which these calls should be handled, must be incorporated in staff training.

For all staff assigned the responsibility of managing telephone calls, as well as physicians, providers, nurses, and the many other persons who may answer a call, training on the telephone system itself is important. In addition to answering a call, include training about establishing and checking voicemails (if applicable) and how to appropriately transfer a call.

Staff Resources

Among the many steps you can take to optimize the telephone in your medical practice, an important one not to overlook is gathering feedback from your staff. Learning how to meet staff needs to do a better job can produce notable improvements in productivity, as well as in job satisfaction and reduced employee turnover. Try these actions:

> ➤ Improve the working conditions for your telephone staff. Discuss equipment needs with staff members. Do they need hands-free headsets? Better chairs? You may avoid future

Workers' Compensation claims by paying attention to ergonomics and buying quality equipment.

- Discuss information needs with staff members. Do they need access to instant messaging to alert the triage nurse that a patient is calling again? Is the EHR system available to them to inform the caller whether a task such as test result notification has been completed? Do they need a training update on the EHR system? Do they need access to the "on-call" list for communication from the hospital? Determine what resources you can deliver to your telephone staff to improve its effectiveness.

- Share telephone data with the telephone operators and triage nurses so they can see the volume of inbound calls they manage, abandonment rates, time on the call, and other similar data. This knowledge permits them to self-manage and work to meet the performance expectations you have defined for telephone work.

Your employees are a wealth of resources. At minimum, on an annual basis, ask each staff member: "What is the one thing that I can get for you for you to do your job better?" You'll be surprised – often pleasantly – about their responses.

BEST PRACTICE

At least once a year, ask each employee: "What is the one thing that I can get for you so that you can do your job better?"

Staff Performance Management

Institute a formal performance management process for telephone staff. The process should be incorporated into daily or weekly feedback for new employees, as well as bi-annual performance reviews for seasoned employees.

- Review performance expectations and data with all staff as they relate to volume and quality. On a routine basis, share these telephone statistics with the staff.
- Evaluate both the quantity of calls and quality of work of the staff involved in call management by listening to recorded calls (if applicable), sampling messages, reviewing the quality of responses and service to patients, and evaluating the turn-around time to respond to messages.
- Hold joint meetings with telephone and practice staff to review call data, scripting, and impacts to scheduling. These meetings can also be a forum to clarify protocols, suggest changes to current policies and procedures, and handle other similar issues so that all recognize their role in meeting the needs of patients.
- Hold staff accountable for meeting service standards (see Chapter 2 for recommended telephone service standards).

Managing the performance of your staff is critical to ensuring that your telephone operations are optimized. You can have the best technology in the world, but you must have the right people with the right knowledge and skills to be successful.

Summary

Staffing the telephones with an appropriate complement of staff with the right skills and training is a prerequisite for telephone success. The employees who answer your telephones are a direct reflection of your practice; these staff members often have more touches with patients than any other staff in the medical practice. Recruit well and provide the training and resources needed for the staff to function at optimal levels, and fully assimilate these staff members into your care team.

End Note

1. For more information on innovative staffing models, see *Innovative Staffing for the Medical Practice* by Deborah Walker Keegan, published by Medical Group Management Association, 2011. This book is available through www.mgma.com or www.amazon.com.

[CHAPTER 5]

Telephone Tools

What the caller hears and how you present yourself on the telephone define the caller's impression of your practice. Experts agree, customers develop their impression of a business within the first 10 seconds, and that's just about the length of time it takes to greet a caller on the telephone. It's your opportunity to make it a great impression, and you can accomplish that with telephone scripts, quality communication, and tools to support your efforts.

In this chapter, we discuss tools and resources to execute a successful telephone operation:

- ➤ Telephone scripts to help ensure consistent, high-quality telephone interactions;
- ➤ Tools to enhance nonverbal communication;
- ➤ Customer service tools to improve service delivery; and
- ➤ Telephone message tools to ensure accurate and complete messages.

BEST PRACTICE

> Print ribbons to hang under your nametags or small signs to adhere to your workstations that say "The First 10 Seconds." This message serves as a reminder of the importance of your initial interaction with the caller.

Telephone Scripts

Use standard telephone scripts to ensure a consistent experience for callers. There are two methods of scripting: (1) design the specific words to say and (2) provide an outline of key information. For a telephone call greeting and closure, which are consistently used in each call, highlight the specific words for staff to say to callers. Given the nature of a medical practice (and the hundreds of reasons that a caller is communicating with you), it's nearly impossible to provide specific scripts for staff to follow for each type of call. Instead, an effective management tool is to provide outlines based on call type of the practice's expectations for the information that should be gathered and/or communicated during the call. As an example, Exhibit 5.1 presents a list of information that should be outlined for appointment-related calls.

[EXHIBIT 5.1] Information to be scripted for appointment calls

- Scripted greeting (see "The greeting" section on p. 97);
- Appointment information (provider, day of week, date, time, and location); repeat this information to the patient at the conclusion of the call;
- Request to complete and submit registration and medical history online, as applicable, while revealing – and repeating – the practice's Website;
- Reminder to bring proper identification, insurance card(s), payment, and referral information;
- Statement of account balance, as applicable, with an offer to accept a credit/debit card payment from the patient if willing and able;
- Preparation instructions for any tests, as applicable;
- Directions (patients may be directed to Website or transferred to an extension that provides automated directions); and
- Scripted closure (see "The closing" section on p. 98).

[EXHIBIT 5.2] **Develop scripts for frequent scenarios**

- Doesn't speak English
- Is having a medical emergency
- Has the wrong number
- Has a clinical question
- Requests a prescription
- Asks to speak with a physician or staff member
- Asks to have results of a test
- Wants to update his or her personal or insurance information
- Wants a copy of his or her medical record
- Wants to discuss his or her bill
- Has a complaint
- Asks personal questions regarding patients (for example, father calls to see if his son is a patient of your practice)

Although the reasons for calls vary, develop written protocols for handling frequent situations, such as those presented in Exhibit 5.2. Give staff members the tools they need to effectively manage each caller.

As Exhibit 5.2 demonstrates, many common questions are asked each day; script responses enable the operator to get right to the point. Directions to the office or referred testing sites, as well as the name of the provider on call, should always be handy. Reinforce the importance of using telephone scripts by incorporating compliance with scripting in your staff performance management process. Provide your staff members with the telephone scripts they need to manage the telephones and then hold them accountable for using these important tools.

BEST PRACTICE

Sample script: "I would be happy to answer your question, and you may find other useful information on our Website at www.practicename.com."

- - -

In addition to scripting common telephone scenarios, train staff to recognize situations in which calls need to be escalated (see Chapter 3) and emergencies. Give staff the guidelines to handle extenuating circumstances with referring physicians. Be sure to provide this training to staff members who you believe would never even answer your telephones – even the lab technician who might pick up a call now and then. We're not suggesting that the lab technician step into the role of your triage nurse, but you never know who will be around when a crisis occurs. An informed staff contributes to ensuring an efficient office. Preparation is good risk management *and* patient service.

BEST PRACTICE

Post answers to common questions on your practice's Website or online patient portal, thereby reducing the need for patients to call you with routine questions.

- - -

If you can anticipate some of the callers' questions, post them with the correct responses on your practice's Website or portal in a "Frequently Asked Questions" section. This may reduce the volume of calls from patients asking routine questions. Whenever appropriate, direct callers to information provided on your practice's Website, online patient portal, or via the patient's personal health record. Although it may take one or two verbal reminders, callers will slowly but surely get in the habit of checking for information online (or wherever you may direct them) instead of calling. Avoiding the need for a call – while still meeting the caller's expectation – is a strategy that promotes the goals of providing consistently good patient service. (See Chapter 3 for more ideas on alternatives to calls.)

BEST PRACTICE

Keep writing tablets near all telephones. As soon as the caller states his or her name, write it down. Otherwise, you may forget the name as you listen to the details of the request, forcing you to ask for the caller's name again at the end of the conversation. The caller may wonder what other information you missed. After you have the name, use it as often as you can during the conversation. The name offers a connection to the patient and demonstrates that you are listening and attentive.

The greeting

Each caller should have a consistently positive experience when telephoning your practice. To ensure uniform and reliable experience for callers, we recommend four elements in the greeting:

1. Welcome: Acknowledge and welcome the caller.

    Example: "Good morning."

2. Identification: State the name of the practice and/or department.

3. Operator's first name

4. Query

    Example: "How may I help you?"

Incorporating these four elements into each greeting is a small but important step that ensures each caller gets a consistently high level of service.

In the greeting, use the full name of your practice, avoiding any slang ("Ped-e-G-I," for example, for a pediatric gastroenterology practice). It may be quicker for your receptionist to say, "Hello, Surg Onc" (as opposed to "Hello, Surgical Oncology Associates"), but you'll lose time in the long run as callers pause and wonder if they've reached the right place. Everyone who answers a telephone should say your practice's name with as few abbreviations as possible. It makes a more professional impression and ultimately contributes to a higher level of service. Remember that this initial greeting is a distinct marketing opportunity to state your brand to every caller, so use the opportunity to express it appropriately and consistently. For example: "Good morning. You have reached Medical Practice Associates. This is Sally speaking. How may I help you?" This should be a routine part of how each telephone call is answered.

The closing

In addition to a consistent greeting, conclude each call with a standard closure. Instruct staff to use the caller's name – "Ms. Jones" or "Mr. Smith," for example – at the end of conversations. Indeed, feel free to use the caller's name several times during the conversation. Stating the patient's name reinforces the fact that you are actively listening.

Go a step further and thank patients for choosing your practice, particularly when scheduling an appointment. Conclude calls by asking callers if there is anything else they need. For example: "Thank you for choosing Medical Practice Associates for your care, Ms. Jones. Is there anything else I can do to help you?" If performed consistently, you'll leave a positive and memorable impression.

BEST PRACTICE

Conclude every call with "Thank you for choosing our practice for your care." It demonstrates your appreciation – and acknowledges the fact that the patient made a choice.

Positive response sets

Although scripts cannot be written for each possible scenario, staff members can be educated to use particular words and phrases. The words they choose when responding to callers should reflect a positive response set rather than a negative one. Scripts also help educate staff to enhanced verbal communication skills. As a service industry, patients do not want to be treated as a number or a disease. Instead, professional, compassionate, and service-oriented behaviors can be taught through repetitive scripting and customer-minded tools.

Review the examples in Exhibit 5.3 with staff while asking for feedback about other positive responses to use – or negative ones to avoid.

BEST PRACTICE

The telephone can leave staff members with the impression that they are somehow detached from patient care. Emphasize that *every telephone call is a life*. Particularly for telephone staff who are not located in the clinical area, hang pictures of patients as a reminder of the important connection that telephone staff members have with patients even when they can't see them face to face.

> **[EXHIBIT 5.3]** Positive response sets

When you cannot provide the caller's desired outcome – there are no earlier openings on the appointment schedule, for example – shift the language from a negative to a positive by informing callers what you can do (vs. what you can't do).

Instead of saying:	"No. I can't help you."
Respond this way:	When a patient calls late in the day with a nonurgent medical question, for example, but the clinical staff has already left the office, reply by saying: "The office staff has left for the day, but they will be in tomorrow morning at 9 a.m., and I will have the nurse contact you at that time. Is the 555.555.5555 number a good one to use or is there a better number to reach you tomorrow?"
Instead of saying:	"Hang on a second."
Respond this way:	"It may take me a few minutes to research this. Are you able to hold while I check or shall I take your number to call you back?"
Instead of saying:	"You'll have to …"
Respond this way:	Give a response that does not appear to tell the patient what he or she has to do. Instead, reply by saying: "Here's how we can help you with that…. Is this acceptable?"
Instead of saying:	"Dr. _____ is not in the office today."
Respond this way:	"Dr. _____ is not in the office today. How may I help you?"
Instead of saying:	"She's at lunch."
Respond this way:	"I am sorry, but she is not available. May I have her call you later or may I be of assistance?"
Instead of:	Ignoring the patient's comments;
Respond this way:	"I am sorry that you are not feeling well," or a similar remark, to acknowledge the patient's comment and, in the event that the patient is upset, to diffuse the situation.

Information requests

Make sure your employees have the requisite knowledge to answer common questions posed by callers. We have witnessed numerous instances where employees have not been given the information to respond to callers. The questions in Exhibit 5.4 reflect the sophistication of today's patients – and the lack of training for many

[EXHIBIT 5.4] **Patient inquiries that require expanded knowledge**

- Which one of the physicians would *you* select for your own healthcare (or your child's)?
- Where did the physician train?
- How many _____ procedures does he (or she) do each year?
- What is his (or her) complication rate for this procedure?
- How much will the procedure cost?

telephone staff members to respond to specific questions regarding the medical practice. Ask your employees to jot down the questions they receive and create standard information protocols for staff to use when responding to patients.

Staff Knowledge

Patients pose many clinical questions when they call your medical practice. To gauge the quality of telephone contact with patients, many practices ask the question: "Is the staff knowledgeable?" as part of their patient satisfaction survey. Although most clinical staff members regard themselves as very informed, educated, and conversant, some patients don't come to that conclusion, particularly during telephone conversations. When a patient asks a question about his or her treatment or test results, it's common for a clinical staff member to respond: "Let me ask Dr. Smith."

It's no surprise that patients are concerned about this staff member's knowledge – he or she never gives information without checking first with the physician. Patients do not differentiate whether the staff member is reluctant to release information without the physician's approval – or just doesn't know the answer. Patients tend to assume it is the latter. Adding to the mix are the frustrations involved with the delays that some patients experience waiting for a return call.

To improve the process, sit down and determine patients' most frequently asked questions. Ask your physicians if they are willing to develop new guidelines or clinical protocols, in writing, that permit clinical staff to respond to some of the patients' inquiries, while also clarifying when the physician should become involved in the issue. For example, basic post-operative wound care could be included in the new guidelines, with the clinical staff providing this education to patients and responding to patients' inquiries regarding their care. So, too, clear guidance should be developed about which questions should be referred to the physician immediately vs. those that can be responded to later in the day.

In addition to the new guidelines, it's important for clinical staff members to change their responses to patients' questions that truly do need the physician's response. In these situations, train the nurses and medical assistants to respond: "That is a very important question, and I know that Dr. Smith would like to hear it. I'd like to run it by him and get back to you." This new response positions the clinical staff as an integral member of the care team. The old way of responding ("Let me ask Dr. Smith") works to perpetuate a reliance on the physician to personally manage all calls rather than engender confidence in the clinical care team.

If your physicians are willing and your clinical team is up to the challenge, these changes in workflow related to telephone calls can improve patient communication and practice efficiency.

Nonverbal Communication Tools

Simply managing the inbound telephone call by imparting consistent information is not sufficient. In fact, we've all had interactions with a person over the telephone where we knew that the information we received was accurate and comprehensive, but the manner in which we received it was totally inappropriate. In groundbreaking research, UCLA Professor Emeritus Albert Mehrabian concluded that only 18 percent of a customer's experience was related to the words used, while an overwhelmingly 82 percent of the caller's experience was defined by the vocal qualities of the operator (see Exhibit 5.5).

By studying and improving your vocal quality, staff can improve each caller's experience with your practice. Ensure that callers feel they are being treated with respect, courtesy, and compassion by focusing on a positive display of the following vocal qualities:

Tone: Expression of feeling or emotion
Rate: Number of words spoken per minute
Inflection: Emphasizing words and syllables to enhance the verbal encounter
Pitch: Highness or deepness of voice
Volume: How loud or soft the voice sounds

[EXHIBIT 5.5] Importance of vocal qualities

Source: Data from UCLA Professor Emeritus Albert Mehrabian. 1981. *Silent Messages: Implicit Communication of Emotions and Attitudes*. Belmont, Calif.: Wadsworth.

Train staff to retain the information about these characteristics by remembering the acronym "TRIPV."

One of the key vocal qualities, the rate of speaking, can convey "urgency" to a voice as if the operator needs to hurry a caller along so they can get to the next caller. This is easily perceived by callers as a lack of interest and "coldness" rather than compassion and caring. It's true that some callers may have a hard time getting to the point. Instead of speaking at a rapid rate, help them along by politely asking, "What may I help you with, Ms. Jones?" during a pause (or even a breath) in their statement. Try role playing during a staff meeting to show staff how to help patients get to the point without being perceived as pushy.

Ask your staff members about examples of positive – and negative – vocal qualities that they have personally experienced. Using these scenarios, as well as ones from your practice, role-play the required tone, rate, inflection, pitch, and volume that you expect of staff.

A bad mood or lousy attitude seems to leap through the telephone. Watch for inadvertent nonverbal communication, such as sighs or moans. Beware of talking too rapidly or loudly as well as using a condescending or inappropriate tone. You can sense someone's attitude through the telephone. Make a point of smiling as you speak – patients will sense that smile – even over the telephone. Try putting a mirror on the wall in front of telephone staff members and ask them to smile sincerely when they answer each call, just as they would be expected to in a face-to-face encounter.

 BEST PRACTICE

You can sense someone's attitude through the telephone. Make a point of smiling as you speak – patients will sense that smile – even over the telephone.

Some people have a natural gift for handling telephone inquiries. Listen to staff members to see who your telephone stars are and turn their skills into staff training so you can start improving everyone's telephone efficiency and service quality.

Customer Service Tools

Beyond the professionalism, courtesy, and empathy perceived by patients when they contact your medical practice, a number of customer service tools can help when interactions with the patient do not go as planned.

These difficult "moments of truth" are often the benchmark that patients use to assess your medical practice's quality. Indeed, for many patients, their assessment of your service serves as a proxy for their perception of your quality. Many patients may not have the knowledge and tools to assess clinical quality, but they certainly have the knowledge and tools to assess your level of service.

Keep your service promise
Make sure staff members understand the importance of keeping their service promise. If the patient is informed that he or she will receive a return call – referred to as a "callback" – in three hours, place the call to the patient in three hours – even if it means that the patient will only be informed of an update rather than a resolution to his or her inquiry. Keeping your service promise reflects on your practice's integrity and influences the confidence patients have in your practice. Plus, it vastly reduces the work associated with repeat calls.

Practice service recovery
A medical practice is a service organization. Although we hope that every interaction with the patient is positive, some fall short of our expectations. When this occurs, be sure to have a ready response

> **[EXHIBIT 5.6] Remuneration for service failures**
>
> A health system requested guidance from the Office of the Inspector General (OIG) regarding the use of gift cards for service failures. The cards are $10 in value, with a limit of $50 per annum, redeemable at certain local vendors, excluding the health system. The program would not be advertised. Historically, the OIG has considered any remuneration to patient as an inducement for referrals. On July 28, 2008, the OIG issued a statement in favor of the gift cards: "we conclude that (i) the Proposed Arrangement would not constitute prohibited remuneration within the meaning of section 1128A(a)(5) of the Act; and (ii) while the Proposed Arrangement could potentially generate prohibited remuneration under the anti-kickback statute, if the requisite intent to induce or reward referrals of Federal health care program business were present, the OIG would not impose administrative sanctions …"
>
> Source: OIG Advisory Opinion No. 08-07.

that is fair and equitable to all callers who experience a problem situation. For example, order a small bouquet of flowers to be delivered to a patient to apologize for the fact they were lost on hold for two hours, or send them a small gift card or a written note of apology. Be sure you do not become extravagant or your gift may be construed as an inducement for referrals to your practice. See Exhibit 5.6 for an advisory opinion from the Office of the Inspector General. Work with your legal counsel and malpractice carrier regarding service recovery that is appropriate for the situation.

Manage complaints

Perhaps the most important response to learn is reacting to a caller's complaint. Instead of being defensive (easy to feel that way because the complaint received by the telephone operator is typically about an issue over which the operator has no control), reply with a positive statement. When a caller complains, make an affirmative statement; for example: "Thank you for bringing that to our attention" or "I'm sorry that we didn't meet your expectations." These statements often diffuse caller frustration, as the caller feels recognized and appreciated.

BEST PRACTICE

When a caller complains, make an affirmative statement such as "Thank you for bringing that to our attention" or "I'm sorry that we didn't meet your expectations." The manager should call every patient who registers a formal complaint. Even if the complaint cannot be resolved, the acknowledgment alone proves to the patient that the practice recognizes its patients' concerns.

- -

Use the patient's name in the conversation; it demonstrates that you are listening. Write down the caller's comments to verbally summarize at the conclusion of the conversation; it indicates that you took the complaint seriously. Many callers just want to be heard. If possible, state the next step that you will take with the complaint; such as giving a note to the physician or nurse. For patients who want an answer to their complaint, give realistic expectations about response times.

If the caller has a complaint about your practice or is simply taking out their bad mood on you, don't absorb their emotions. Help staff resist the urge to respond negatively. Post a quote, photo, or some other calming focal point at staff workstations. It will give them something to focus on when difficult situations arise. Provide a script that is easy for the staff to remember, such as "thank you for bringing that to our attention, Ms. Jones."

Also, give staff a process for escalating the call to a manager and the scripting to permit this smooth transition of a disgruntled caller. For example, consider the following script: "Thank you for bringing this to our attention. I want to be sure my manager has an opportunity to talk with you directly about this issue. Are you able to hold for two minutes while I locate her or can I have her call you back within the next 30 minutes?" This works to diffuse some of the caller's emotion by signifying to the caller the importance of the issue or complaint but also buys some time to allow the caller to calm down. After the manager has called the patient to review the complaint, he or she should record the patient's name, date, time, and issue for the practice's leadership to review. Incorporating complaints about the telephone (and other issues) in a standard log provides a basis to discover and address the root causes of complaints and to understand the roles the practice's staff, processes, or equipment may play in creating or failing to sufficiently resolve the situation. The manager should call *every* patient who registers a formal complaint. Even if the complaint cannot be resolved, the acknowledgment alone proves to the patient that the practice is interested in its patients' concerns.

Foster teamwork

Patients can readily perceive dysfunction in a medical practice, and it can play a large role in patient assessment of your telephone service. For example, if a telephone operator handles repeat calls from a patient throughout the day and informs the patient that it is the clinical staff's fault for not promptly returning his or her calls, telephone operators are sharing the internal dysfunction of a medical practice. The importance of teamwork should not be overlooked. The level of patient satisfaction typically mirrors the level of staff satisfaction. Make sure your medical practice is functioning as a true care team.

Message-Taking Tools

Your employees need the skills and tools to take accurate and complete telephone messages. Telephone message pads should feature templates with boxes to check off (if manual) or point and click (if electronic) to improve message quality and staff efficiency. Everyone whose duties include answering a telephone should know basic medical terminology and be adept at correctly spelling important medical terms that describe chief complaints, diagnoses, medications, and other common medical issues. Indecipherable messages force you to call back patients, pharmacies, laboratories, or other physicians to figure out what they said. Returning calls to patients (or other callers) simply to request clarification of the initial message constitutes rework, which is costly for your medical practice. It also leads to caller frustration and the perception that your practice is inefficient.

Why take a message?

The first important step to efficient message handling is to eliminate unnecessary messages wherever it is possible and appropriate to do so. For example, a scheduler can be delegated the authority to make a decision regarding a same-day visit request without having to take a message and run it by the physician. Nurses, medical assistants, and other clinical associates can be given their own business cards, which can be handed to patients along with a personal introduction and communication that he or she can provide needed assistance if the patient has questions, thereby avoiding unnecessary messages for providers. It's a small investment that helps create credibility. By empowering your staff, you reduce the time-consuming steps of taking, transmitting, and responding to messages, and, just as important, patients gain confidence in the practice.

Physicians can help this process along. A physician's verbal assurance to the patient that his or her clinical associate, or the practice's health coach or patient navigator, is an important member of your team helps patients feel comfortable communicating with a team member. This also reduces the volume of telephone calls by patients who state: "I only want to talk with my doctor." A team approach to patient care and to managing inbound calls is becoming the norm.

Finally, ask your staff members to sit down and record the questions that are most frequently asked of them. Gather the physician's input to the question, and you're ready to go. Staff can confidently respond to questions based on the written guidelines. Don't overstep the bounds of knowledge, however. If a patient has a question or need that is beyond the scope of expertise of the clinical assistant or nurse, they should not try to answer the question. But neither should they just revert to saying, "I need to ask Dr. Smith." Instead, respond: "That is an excellent question, Ms. Walters. I'd like to run that question by Dr. Smith. Where can I reach you when I call back?" Then query the physician, and call the patient back with a response in a timely manner.

Message completeness

Accurate and complete messages are essential to an efficient office. In either paper or electronic templates, develop sample messages to respond to each of the following telephone inquiries:

- Test result requests;
- Medication renewals;
- Frequently asked questions of the nurse;
- Same-day appointment requests;
- Scheduling appointments when the patient has not been seen for a pre-defined period of time; and
- Other common requests to your practice.

During new employee training, review the sample messages, pointing out the essential components of each and make sure your staff members are consistently taking accurate and complete messages by auditing their messages in comparison to the samples.

Use the telephone tracking worksheet discussed in Chapter 2 to focus on topics to educate staff members so they can improve their message-taking skills. Ensure that this education includes appropriate follow-up questions that employees should ask to determine the reason for the call and ensure that they garner sufficient detail about the issue. Develop scripts regarding common patient inquiries so that suitable follow-up questions and details are obtained for an accurate and complete message, and that an appropriate determination is made regarding the urgency of the call and its subject matter.

For the majority of calls, this step increases the likelihood that the call can be managed without the need for an outbound call to the patient to request clarification.

Missed messages

Documentation of every telephone call is vital. Emphasize to staff and providers that every telephone call represents a patient's life. Failure to record a message is simply not acceptable. In addition to documenting all messages, ensure that all messages are responded to within a defined time period. With an EHR system, the message can be seamlessly attached to the patient's record. In a paper system, however, tools are needed to make sure all messages are tracked. One method is to take messages on a duplex pad. Keep one copy with the pad, thereby creating a running log of all inbound calls. File the original message in the patient's chart by taping it inside the chart. Another method is to take messages on paper that has adhesive on one side to facilitate chart filing, while keeping a copy of the message in a folder in the event that the original is lost.

The importance of the process to ensure that all communication is documented and responded to cannot be underestimated. Message-taking is a risk management issue that needs to be given high priority. Discuss your protocols with the practice administrator, medical director, and the director(s) assigned to internal risk management, as well as your malpractice liability carrier to make sure that your processes meet quality standards.

BEST PRACTICE

> Documentation and appropriate management of every telephone call are vital. Emphasize to staff and providers that every telephone call represents a patient's life.

How to reach patients

A key step in taking a message is to determine how to return the caller's telephone inquiry. When taking messages, urge staff to recognize the importance of accurately recording patients' telephone numbers to permit calls to be returned in a timely manner. Gather a "best" callback number from the caller, and always request an alternate as well. For example, "Is 555.5555 the *best* number to reach you at today? Is there another number that we can use to contact you in case we can't reach you at the first number you gave us?" Use the patient's call as an opportunity to review the telephone numbers on file for the patient. This allows your staff to perform a quick, but very helpful registration update to correct the telephone number in the registration portion of the patient's account.

BEST PRACTICE

Embrace communication methods that do not require synchronous work. The use of an online patient portal, secure e-mail message, or text message shifts work to platforms that are more efficient and minimizes inbound telephone calls.

As discussed in Chapter 3, proactively ask patients to use technology to communicate. During the message-taking and/or callback process, for example, providers and staff can encourage patients to use the practice's online patient portal. E-mail and/or text messaging may also be an option, with the patient's written permission. These means of communication do not require synchronous communication; shifting work to platforms that are more efficient for your practice to manage minimizes telephone calls to and from your practice – and saves significant resources.

Alternatives to message-taking

If your employees are taking a high volume of messages, explore other avenues to manage calls without the need for a message. For example, use the management techniques we described in Chapter 3 to minimize inbound call demand. Or consider whether it is time for a telephone nurse triage and advice unit to directly manage clinical calls without the need for an initial step that involves a nonclinical person taking a message. Or perhaps your practice can create secure electronic messaging with patients to permit them to submit their inquiries in writing to the practice, thereby eliminating the need for a telephone call – and a message to be taken.

First-call resolution

To fundamentally improve efficiency and reduce resources that must be allocated to your telephones, set a goal of first-call resolution. Instead of taking a message and playing the game of telephone tag, develop a protocol so that callers' needs are met during their *initial* call. That is, the caller gets to the right person and his or her request for information is satisfied in real time. Indeed, the act of message-taking is not an insignificant process. In fact, it is quite costly. Our research reveals that each message, on average, costs $15, and other experts have estimated the cost to exceed $30 per message. At minimum, before a message is even taken, require staff members to ask: "Is there anything that *I* can do to help you?" Although not all calls can be resolved this way, this protocol definitely reduces the number of messages that must be taken. Staff training is an essential component of this strategy; the ability of the employee to provide accurate and thorough information, and to be competent at handling the patient's questions and problems, is a significant driver of patient satisfaction. First-call resolution is predicated on the ability of employees to be capable of handling the call to completion without requiring assistance via a transferred call or a subsequent call. Avoiding these transfers or subsequent calls translates into higher efficiency and better service.

BEST PRACTICE

Set a goal of first-call resolution. Every message costs your practice, on average, $15.

Allowing the appropriate staff member to get the job done on the caller's first communication is perhaps the greatest asset that an EHR can offer to your operations. With the patient's information immediately available, the needs of many callers – from patients to referring physicians – can be handled more expeditiously. If you have an EHR, make sure you take advantage of the tools that maximize your practice's ability to provide first-call resolution to callers.

Callbacks

Callbacks is a term commonly used by practices to describe return calls to patients and other callers. To maintain the high-level customer service you expect to deliver, as well as to appropriately manage internal risk, the callback process needs to be effectively managed. Develop guidelines for providers and staff regarding callbacks, including:

- Protocols for physician-to-physician callbacks;
- Establishment and adherence to turnaround time for patient callbacks; and
- Protocols to enhance the use of technology.

These considerations are reviewed, in detail, in the sections that follow.

Physician-to-physician calls

To reduce callbacks to referring physicians, expedite physician-to-physician communication. The time it consumes to record a message from a physician who calls, route the message to the physician, allow the physician time to review the message, play telephone tag, and, finally, reach the originating physician not only adds delays to the process, but it also is very expensive – for both physicians! Several options can be considered as you work to streamline physician-to-physician calls.

Each staff member must make a judgment as to whether or not to interrupt the physician to take a telephone call. To avoid problems in varying judgments that may frustrate staff and providers, develop written guidelines as to if and when to interrupt the physician. Ensure that physicians agree with the guidelines and make sure the staff understands how to interpret the guidelines. Remember, every one of these calls is vital to your patients' care, so guidance is essential.

To streamline physician-to-physician communication, consider creating a separate telephone number or extension for referring physicians to use. Communicate this number to your referring physicians and determine one of the following methods to manage the inbound physician caller:

- The telephone (or extension) is immediately answered by the telephone operators, with the caller directly connected to the physician or that physician's nurse. The telephone system may be configured such that these calls are given priority in the queue.

- The telephone rings with a distinct tone at all stations in the suite (often referred to as a "bat telephone," red telephone, or presidential line) and each member of the staff is instructed to immediately answer those telephone calls if they are free to do so.

- A cellular or mobile telephone with a distinct number or extension is held by a nurse (often rotating on a weekly basis); the nurse assigned to the telephone answers the call and discusses the immediacy of the issue with the physician caller.
- A cellular or mobile telephone with a distinct number or extension is held by the physician on call who immediately responds to the caller.
- A cellular or mobile telephone with a distinct number or extension is held by a physician; the responsibility is rotated among physicians on a weekly basis, thereby creating immediate access to a physician in the practice when referring physicians call.
- A central call center is established to process all inbound referring physician calls, particularly relevant for physician practices that are tasked with handling a very high volume of these calls.

We have witnessed successful implementation of each of the above options; however, as accountable care and collaborative care models are developed, the preferred model is to create a direct communication channel between physicians that does not rely on the synchronous communication required by the telephone. Instead, encourage referring physicians to correspond with your practice's physicians through a secure electronic method. This may be a part of the existing EHR system; a community or health system–based health information exchange; an online patient portal with functionality to accommodate referring physician communication; or perhaps a custom, secure electronic interchange engineered specifically for that purpose. Regardless of the platform, determining a better means of exchanging and documenting information between physicians should be a priority.

To reduce callbacks, as well as offer a value-added service, some medical practices have created a virtual consult capability. Let's review a case example of virtual consults:

> ■ CASE STUDY ■
>
> **Dr. Joseph Reece**
>
> Dr. Joseph Reece, a primary care physician, suspects his patient has broken her wrist and takes a digital X-ray. He communicates with Dr. Shuman, the hand surgeon who is on call for virtual consults, transmitting the clinical documentation and the digital X-ray to the surgeon. Together, Drs. Reece and Shuman determine the next steps for the patient.

This "virtual consult"– the availability of a physician assigned to provide consult capability on a given day – improves not only communication between physicians, but it enhances the timeliness to care. It is likely that this model of physician-to-physician "on-demand" communication will increase with time.

Callback protocols

Patients communicate with your medical practice every hour of every day. Message-taking, as discussed previously, is an important aspect of managing these calls, but those messages must not only be taken, but also handled to fruition. To manage the calls, practices must establish and adhere to a turnaround time for patient callbacks.

Callbacks are not always handled in a timely manner. If the call isn't returned to the patient in a time frame in which the patient believes is appropriate, the patient calls again. Repeat calls from patients are a significant source of opportunity for improvement, as patients initiate repeat calls to your practice when they do not receive a timely response to their initial inquiries. When the amount of staff time required to handle these calls is taken into account, repeat calls from patients can be a substantial, and mostly unnecessary, component of operating costs. Each of the following scenarios generates a high volume of repeat calls:

- Calls immediately go to voicemail; the caller is unsure if the message is picked up or when to expect a response.
- Patients are told to "give us a call to let us know how you are doing," but the message isn't retrieved. Thinking that the request is an important instruction, as it was communicated by their physician, patients call and call again trying to get through.
- A busy nurse doesn't check his or her voicemail until the end of the day. During the day, multiple messages from the same patient pile up.
- A message is taken by the telephone operator, but the caller does not have confidence that the operator understood his or her issue or took an appropriate message, so the patient calls back and leaves another message.
- A message is taken by the telephone operator; however, the caller has not been given a time frame in which to expect a return telephone call.

BEST PRACTICE

Eliminate or dramatically reduce the use of voicemail. Voicemail is simply a method of batching and delaying the work. Instead, create real-time, one-touch strategies to respond to callers.

Your medical practice can reduce the number of repeat calls from patients by implementing one or more of the following actions:

- Perform first-call resolution. Handle the patient's needs without having to take a message or call the patient back.
- Decrease the circumstances that lead to unnecessary calls.
- Eliminate or dramatically reduce the use of voicemail. Voicemail is simply a method to batch and delay work. Instead, create real-time, one-touch strategies that permit patients to receive information during their initial call.

➤ Separate the work of the patient visit from the work of the telephones, getting the telephones "off stage." As we discussed in Chapter 4, How to Staff Your Telephones, this is the preferred model for staffing the telephones. This ensures that there is a dedicated, focused staff to manage the telephones, thereby reducing time delays and avoiding repeat calls.

➤ Ensure that telephone operators have the knowledge and communication skills to manage message-taking capability in a manner that engenders confidence. If not, the caller is likely to question the competency of the operator – the caller just does not have confidence that the operator took a complete message and gave it to the intended party, much less remembered to return the call when, or if, an answer is obtained. The result? The patient calls again, quite likely before the message has even reached the intended party.

➤ Inform the patient regarding when he or she should expect a return call. Meet with your staff and develop a standard time frame by which all calls are returned. In this fashion, the caller is notified that he or she will receive a callback within three hours, for example, and can plan for that time delay. Then keep the service promise and be sure to place the return call to the patient within the three-hour window. Even if the inquiry is not resolved in that time frame, place the return call and notify the patient of the status of his or her inquiry. This helps prevent the person from calling back, again and again, asking the same question. Consider reviewing industry norms for callbacks, such as the one presented in Exhibit 5.7 from URAC when establishing your service expectations.

BEST PRACTICE

Establish a service promise – a turnaround time – for callbacks.

> **[EXHIBIT 5.7] Clinical call turnaround**
>
> Washington, D.C.-based URAC, an independent, nonprofit organization that accredits and certifies healthcare organizations, provides accreditation for Health Call Centers. One of its standards is a turnaround time averaging 30 minutes for a clinical staff person to respond to clinical triage communications.
>
> Source: www.urac.org/programs/prog_accred_hcc_ss.aspx?navid=accreditation&pagename=prog_accred_HCC. Accessed August 20, 2012.

There's nothing more frustrating to a customer than unmet expectations. If you tell the patient to expect a test result in five days, then you need to communicate the result within those five days. Better yet, tell them to expect five days and then deliver in three days. Delight patients by setting appropriate expectations. Develop reasonable expectations that you can always beat by discussing the common time frames that you will give to patients for test results notification, prescription renewals, surgery scheduling, referral processing, and physician or nurse callbacks. Distribute the expectations to providers and staff, and incorporate them into patient materials and your practice's Website. Never set an expectation you can't beat. Exceeding your own expectations creates delighted customers; failing to meet them is a recipe for disaster.

Many medical practices have established a daily cutoff time for inbound calls and callbacks. Patients who call the medical practice during the last hour of office hours are informed that unless the issue is urgent, they will not receive a return call until the next business day. Note that many of these calls during the last hour are repeat calls; the caller simply has not received a timely response and is now in limbo.

Although a cutoff time for callbacks is routinely used in many medical practices, it is likely not sustainable in the near future, as medical practices become part of accountable care networks, participate in patient-centered medical homes, and embrace similar value-based approaches to healthcare delivery. In place of the traditional 9-to-5 approach to patient access to nonemergency services, 24/7 access for patients is becoming the new, expected way of doing business. Feeding these expectations of instant access is the portability of healthcare information that an EHR affords.

BEST PRACTICE

A cutoff time for callbacks is likely not sustainable in the future; 24/7 access capability is the new, expected way of doing business.

Some options to consider for your medical practice include:

- Work with your hospital to establish a 24/7 nurse triage line, with the nurse triage staff receiving access to the patients' medical records or working from established clinical protocols.
- Inform your answering service to transfer all calls at the end of day and after hours to a physician, advanced practice provider, or nurse from your practice who can respond to the patient in real time.
- Determine the need for an answering service; it may make more sense for your practice to have a nurse or advanced practice provider to take "live calls" from patients at the end of the day or after hours. Studies have shown that when physicians give out their home or cellular telephone number to patients, it is rarely abused.
- Educate your patients so they can recognize the urgency of their medical situation. This enables them to understand the best action to take, for example, when a telephone call vs. a secure e-mail message to the care team is most appropriate.
- Extend office hours to accommodate patients in the office, face to face. Seek remuneration for these visits, including the

enhanced reimbursement that some insurance companies offer for after-hours care.[1]

➤ Establish performance expectations for all staff in the medical practice; if a call is received at the end of day, a staff member is given the responsibility to manage that call, including responding to the caller with an answer or a status update. Consider migrating your staff to an expanded workweek (for example, if they currently work 32 hours, expand to 36 hours) or flexing the hours of staff work (for example, variable shifts) to accommodate patients but avoid paying overtime.

In addition to calls from physicians and patients, your medical practice likely receives a high call volume from vendors, pharmacies, hospitals, and a host of other stakeholders. Managing callbacks to these entities depends on the urgency of the issue, as judged by the initial party who takes the call. Some of these calls will be transferred from a telephone operator to a nurse or manager to handle the issue, particularly if the call is of a clinical nature and urgent or time-sensitive. For example, the hospital admissions department has a question about a planned next-day admission or an important piece of equipment has broken and the vendor needs to determine whether a replacement unit is needed and when.

Other calls, however, are less urgent and a message can be taken and either sent to the appropriate inbox when electronic messaging is employed or a handwritten message can be taken and delivered to the party. For these calls, it is also important to establish a service expectation for the practice. For example, you may establish a policy that all nonphysician or nonpatient callers receive a callback no later than the end of the following day that their call is received. In this fashion, you can notify callers when to expect a return call, thereby avoiding repeat calls for the same issue – and at the same time position your practice for service delivery.

Take the opportunity to manage the callback process to avoid generating repeat calls. These calls tie up staff time unnecessarily and foster caller frustration – and even anger.

Summary

Your practice is evaluated each and every day by patients in the few minutes they interact with your staff via the telephone. Ensure that your employees have the tools they need to delight callers, to include telephone scripts and tools to enhance customer service, message-taking, and callbacks. Evaluate the work tools provided to the staff to identify opportunities to streamline work and/or leverage technology. Appropriate telephone call handling tactics should become part of your practice's essential staff training and performance management process. Your efforts to eliminate repeat calls and optimize callbacks from your medical practice are critical to keeping your service promise.

End Note

1. See CPT® codes 99050 and 99051. Comply with documentation and coding guidelines. CPT © 2013 American Medical Association. All rights reserved.

CHAPTER 6

Telephone Systems

If telephone operations are on your mind, don't overlook the hardware and software of your telephone system. Managing the people and processes surrounding the telephones is important; however, achieving your goals is also dependent on the telephone system itself. Your telephone system may need new features or you may need to learn more about its existing features to optimize performance.

Several features for each telephone system need to be assessed. Although you may not need all of the functions that telephone system vendors offer, it's important to recognize the possibilities. As your practice changes, particularly if it is growing, it is likely that you will need to increase your system's functionality.

In this chapter, we discuss opportunities to understand and enhance the use of your telephone system to include:

- Effectively using voicemail and automatic call distributors (ACDs);
- Determining the considerations for selecting a system;
- Embracing opportunities to deploy telephony; and
- Recognizing the common functions available in a telephone system.

A multitude of functional options is now available for practices to employ in their telephone system; let's first review the most popular options: voicemail and the ACD.

Voicemail

Voicemail allows callers to communicate with employees at a time when they are busy or otherwise not available. The technology allows a caller to leave a verbal message in a voicemail box that can be later accessed by the user. The box is typically secured by a passcode that must be entered when the user wants to listen to the message.

Not everyone appreciates voicemail, however. Like an auto attendant, a complex voicemail system can easily frustrate callers. Even when you have the best intentions and the system is installed properly, voicemail can waste staff time, frustrate patients and referring physicians, and destroy your practice's service reputation.

If your medical practice decides to use voicemail, establish a written policy for it, including who, how, and when voicemail messages are retrieved. Exhibit 6.1 outlines a sample voicemail policy statement that you can use as a starting point for your medical practice. Establish a time frame for message retrieval, and monitor compliance with it. We recommend that all voicemail boxes be checked, at minimum, each hour. Each voicemail box should be assigned to a person who is accountable for managing the voicemail in accordance with the practice's expectations. All messages should be documented in the EHR or in the practice's established messaging system. Define a specific process for recording information from voicemail into the patient's record or account and hold staff accountable to follow that process when handling voicemail responses.

 BEST PRACTICE

> If you use voicemail, create formal policies and procedures related to its use. Voicemail should be used sparingly and should not be used to screen calls or avoid answering the telephones.

> **[EXHIBIT 6.1] Voicemail sample policy statement**
>
> **Policy Statement:** All telephones should be answered professionally, courteously, and promptly during normal business hours. Voicemail should be used sparingly, such as during high peak telephone demand and/or when a staff member is temporarily away from his or her work area. Voicemail should not be used to screen telephone calls or to avoid answering calls.

Greeting

Each voicemail greeting should be professional and brief, yet it should also provide enough information for the caller to make an informed decision regarding whether or not to leave a voicemail message. Include the following standard elements: professional greeting, name, information for urgent access, invitation for caller to leave a message, and expected response time. Account for the statements made in the automated attendant so as not to repeat the same information in the voicemail message. If, for example, the patient has heard "please hang up and dial 9-1-1 in the event of an emergency," do not repeat this statement in the voicemail greeting unless otherwise instructed by your attorney or malpractice carrier.

BEST PRACTICE

> Be sure your voicemail greeting is pleasant, appropriate in tone and speed, and concise yet instructive.

• •

Sample voicemail greeting:

> *"Hello, this is Susan Green. I am Dr. Smith's nurse and you have reached my voicemail. If this is during normal working hours and you need immediate assistance, please dial "0" and ask for the operator. Today is Monday, June 1, and I am in a meeting until*

> 1 p.m. If you would like to leave a message, please leave your name, telephone number, and brief reason for your call, and I will return calls today between 1 and 5 p.m."

Your greeting should be pleasant, appropriate in tone and speed, and concise yet instructive. For lines where patients may leave messages of a clinical nature, be sure the greeting message instructs patients to seek a live operator if the need is emergent or to dial 9-1-1 if the issue is potentially life threatening. (Check with your attorney or malpractice carrier for a recommended statement.) Of course, the prompts that patients hear should identify the person or department at which the caller is asked to leave his or her message. Update your voicemail greeting on a regular basis to ensure that the caller has the information needed to make an informed decision regarding whether or not to leave a voicemail based on your availability.

Retrieval and response

Staff members are responsible for retrieving voicemail promptly. Voicemail should be retrieved on a routine basis, preferably every 30 minutes and no less than once per hour. If the voicemail is from a patient or concerns a patient's care, the communication should be documented in the patient's record. The nature of the message should be recorded, as well as the time, date, and, if applicable, person who left the message. As with documenting any message, the caller's return telephone number should be recorded.

Responding to a voicemail, like any message, should be considered a priority. All telephone calls should be returned promptly within three hours unless the voicemail greeting indicates a longer absence. Even if the caller's issue has not been resolved, a return call should be made by the end of the three-hour period to inform the caller that the message has been received and to provide an update regarding the action that is planned or has been taken, with a new turnaround time provided to the caller. (See Chapter 5 for more information on callbacks.)

Privacy

Callers have a right to a reasonable expectation of privacy. Voicemail messages should be considered confidential and should not be forwarded without the caller's permission.

Advantages and disadvantages

Is voicemail a time-saver or a time-waster in your practice? It's likely the latter if this 12-step scenario sounds familiar:

1. A patient calls your practice.
2. The receptionist who answers asks the caller to briefly describe her problem or question.
3. The receptionist transfers the patient to the correct staff member – in this case, a nurse.
4. Unfortunately, the nurse is elsewhere, so her voicemail answers the call.
5. The caller again describes her inquiry to the voicemail box.
6. After clinic concludes at 5:30 that evening, the nurse dials into the voicemail system to retrieve his messages.
7. He enters his password.
8. Then he wades through a menu of options, such as, "Press 1 for new messages" and "Press 2 to hear saved messages."
9. He listens to the patient's inquiry (often, a lengthy message during which he takes notes), noting that there are three messages from the same patient, each with a growing sense of urgency in the patient's voice. (If the receptionist who originally took the call also communicated a message, there would also be a fourth message for the nurse to review.)
10. He writes down the patient's telephone number – usually given at the very end of the message – and then deletes the messages from the system.
11. Then he calls the patient (add at least one more step if the nurse decides to assign the callback to someone else), but the patient is not at the callback number. He leaves a message.

12. Finally, the nurse gets the patient on the line and the entire inquiry is repeated. The patient is exasperated by having to leave multiple messages. By now, the patient has thought of a few more questions to ask, and, given the delay in response, is expecting a significant amount of time to be spent fulfilling her needs.

Voicemail, as in the previous scenario, is actually quite inefficient. Consider the time that you spend to access the system, to listen to the lengthy messages callers leave (and which they repeat again when you reach them), and, most importantly, the time it takes to track down the caller. One telephone call consumes countless minutes – minutes that you don't have to spare, and ones that only seem to frustrate callers.

Now, consider this alternative: the patient calls, asks a question, and you answer it. Sounds impossible? With the proliferation of EHR systems, callers can be assisted on the initial response and first-call resolution can be performed because information is instantaneously accessible.

BEST PRACTICE

Develop a goal of first-time resolution for all calls. This may require consideration of how calls are routed and to whom, but avoiding voicemail increases efficiency.

Better yet, eliminate the demand for voicemail altogether by directing patients to message you via your secure electronic messaging system or through your online patient portal. (See Chapter 3 for more tips on reducing the demand for telephone calls.) It's likely that voicemail will soon be a vestige of the past, like the rotary telephone, but it's an important process to manage wisely in the meantime.

If you are considering adding or expanding voicemail, first determine your needs and uses for it. Evaluate voicemail use for each functional area of your practice, including billing, referrals, scheduling, and clinical. Voicemail works best for the nonclinical functions of your practice, or at least those where there won't be an emergency that may lead to a bad outcome. These nonemergent uses for voicemail include billing, referral requests, and business issues. Although calls to these areas should be answered promptly, setting them aside for a short period should not lead to a risk management problem.

Regardless of the functional area, if you determine that voicemail is appropriate for an employee with telephone responsibilities, it should not be used to screen calls. Don't let staff use voicemail as a secretarial service. They may be on other calls, but in some cases they are just in the middle of another task or don't want the interruption of a call. Some might even purposely use voicemail to screen calls. Make a simple rule: Pick up the telephone if you're not already on another call (and can't put that caller on hold to answer the other line or have it routed to an operator); use voicemail only when you're *not* available. Using voicemail for time-shifting – batching return calls to be made on your own time – doesn't increase efficiency. You actually end up busier than ever.

BEST PRACTICE

> Make a simple rule: Pick up the telephone if you're not already on another call (and can't put that caller on hold to answer the other line or have it routed to an operator); use voicemail only when you're not available.

Some practices have banned voicemail. Employees are required to answer incoming calls and patients are rewarded with faster turnaround times for communicating via secure electronic messaging. An alternative to eliminating it altogether is to use it only during specific times, such as turning on the voicemail function during a staff meeting.

Basic functions

Determine how a voicemail system indicates that a message is waiting. Is there a blinking light, an LCD (liquid crystal diode) display, or other visual cue to tell you there's a new message in the system? Some systems can be integrated into the computer network to send e-mails to assigned staff when new messages are waiting, perhaps even converting those voicemails to written messages using voice recognition software. Train staff and supervisors how to identify pending messages.

When choosing a voicemail system, consider its reporting capabilities. Sample activity reports should include the number of messages recorded, total length of messages, and average time before a message is deleted. These functions help you monitor the workload of your staff, as well as how your staff responds to messages from patients and referring physicians.

Make sure that the system's port size and storage capacity are adequate for your needs. For example, how many messages can the voicemail system hold? How long of a message can callers leave? What happens when the system is full? Will staff be alerted or must they depend on patients to tell them that a voicemail box is not accepting new messages? The more sophisticated the reporting, the more effective you will be at managing the system.

Choose a system with interactive voice response (IVR) software that recognizes and adapts to usage patterns. Sophisticated IVR systems can route calls from one of your top referring physicians, for example, straight to your clinical manager.

Avoid a stand-alone voicemail system because it does not allow users to return to a menu after they leave their voicemail message. As with a poorly designed auto attendant, voicemail that is not integrated with the rest of the telephone system may bounce users from an extension where no one picks up, then to the greeting message, back to another unattended extension, return to the greeting, and so on – a potentially endless cycle, and one that could drive away patients, referring physicians, and anyone else who calls. Always give callers an option to reach an operator instead of leaving a voicemail message.

Staff training

Training staff to use the system is as important as the system itself. When selecting a system, scrutinize the vendor's training materials in addition to checking references and the vendor's customer service reputation. Is online training, such as a Web tutorial, available? Training materials should be comprehensive yet quick and simple to use. Include training on the voicemail system as a key component of new staff orientation. Make proficiency on the system a component of performance evaluations for the appropriate staff, as well as orientation for new staff.

Voicemail doesn't always increase practice efficiency and may actually harm it if improperly deployed. As you migrate communication away from the telephones to alternative communication channels, think of voicemail more as a back-up mechanism during peaks of heavy volume or special circumstances. Make voicemail work for you, not against you.

Automatic Call Distributor

An automatic call distributor (ACD) – or a product with similar functionality called a uniform call distributor (UCD) – distributes incoming calls within the practice. The ACD software recognizes busy lines and places callers in waiting queues, distributing the calls to specific lines when they become free. Essentially, an ACD creates the opportunity for you to better route, handle, and categorize calls without requiring an operator to do so. A closely related technology, the automated attendant, allows the telephone call to be "answered" automatically before it is routed through the distribution system.

BEST PRACTICE

> Spend time planning for your automatic call distributor. It can create the opportunity to better route, handle, and categorize calls; however, it can also backfire and frustrate callers if it is not well managed.

An ACD, combined with an automated attendant, replaces the need for a staff member to respond and route telephone calls. After listening to a greeting and instructions, callers can route calls themselves by choosing options such as "Press 1 to schedule an appointment," "Press 2 to renew a prescription," "Press 3 to request a test result," and so forth. Callers and internal users should be able to identify and reach their destinations easily in just one or two steps.

When unmanaged, ACDs can backfire, just like poorly executed voicemail systems. One way in which these systems may backfire results when an internal stakeholder overreacts to the negative responses of what is often a small, but vocal, subset of patients who are unhappy with the automation in general. A physician or employee may react by giving out the practice's "back line" telephone number. Before long, the "back line" becomes a main line. Thus, the technology's cost savings are never realized as the practice struggles to manage these new, unexpected points of telephone entry.

Although many patients expect to encounter ACDs and attendants when calling credit card companies, banks, airlines, and government offices, they place higher demands on their physician's office. Patients interact with their physicians on a much more personal level than they do with other businesses, and they are disappointed when it sounds like a computer is answering their physician's telephone. As time goes by, more patients are adjusting to this reality of a modern medical practice – unless, that is, the technology is executed poorly. Even so, practices in rural areas where small, independent medical practices are still the norm or those with a large senior patient panel might continue to reject this technology because too many of their patients feel it is impersonal and difficult to use. Of course, if you have the resources to invest, using a staff member to personally greet and respond to callers, as well as to distribute their calls, is ideal.

When evaluating ACD systems, be sure to understand the storage capabilities of the system and what happens to call overflow as well as the features listed in Exhibit 6.2.

ACD options

If you decide to use an ACD and attendant, create a clear and concise greeting and limit the number of options to avoid confusing the caller. We recommend the following:

> *Thank you for calling Medical Practice Associates. If this is an emergency, please hang up and dial 9-1-1. Please press one of the following options so we can best direct your call to meet your needs:*

Press 1: To schedule or cancel an appointment
Press 2: To renew a prescription
Press 3: To request a test result
Press 4: To speak with a nurse
Press 5: To discuss your bill

Please press 0 for all other calls or to speak with an operator.

Practices may be able to combine options 2, 3, and/or 4. If more options are needed, consider sub-menus so that the main choices are limited to five. However, limit the sub-menu to one per choice so that callers can reach their destination with no more than two menu options.

Using the selections, a caller should be able to route his or her call to a staff member or staffing unit responsible to manage calls in each specific area with the goal of first-call resolution. Calls that are included on the options menu should be either directed to a specific person(s) or a different strategy should apply; don't fall into the trap of using this technology to simply count your call types.

[EXHIBIT 6.2] **Features of an ACD**

- Expandability
- Flexibility
- Wallboard support (displays incoming calls on a screen)
- Operators can transfer callers to an auto attendant
- Callers can opt in or out of "queue" (and return to a live operator or another menu)
- Silent monitoring
- Operators can log in and out
- Report generation

We recommend that you list no more than five options so callers don't lose track – and patience. Moreover, if using sub-menus, recognize that the patient should not have to choose more than two options to reach a live person. Patients do not get mad at automated attendants; they get mad at feeling trapped and not reaching the right person.

BEST PRACTICE

> List no more than five options on your automated attendant; and if using sub-menus, the caller should not have to choose more than two options to reach a live person.

Furthermore, provide frequent callers a number that moves them to the right party from the beginning of the call. For example, give referring physicians a specific number that moves them directly to a live person. Consider promoting a campaign such as "Dial 9 to save time" for referring physicians to ensure that the adoption of an ACD doesn't prevent their calls from being handled expeditiously.

BEST PRACTICE

> Patients don't get mad at automated attendants; they get mad at feeling trapped and not reaching the right person. Before going live on the system, test the technology and make sure it is working as intended.

For your prompts, don't use an automated voice, ask a staff member (or hire a professional) who has a positive voice presence to record the greeting and options. Importantly, be sure that your options are presented in order. Consider offering choices to non-English-speaking callers, depending on your patient population. Before you go live, test the technology yourself.

If you have determined that the technology isn't right for your general telephone line, consider its application for other situations such as in the business office, as a "back-up" for busy operators, for personal calls to staff members, or for reaching a referral coordinator.

Voicemail can be integrated with an ACD and attendant, allowing callers to leave a message at their chosen option if the requested staff member is unavailable. If you choose this option, make sure it's user-friendly and allows your callers to choose "0" to reach the operator because some people prefer to speak to an operator or don't know which option they should choose.

System Selection

When selecting a new telephone system, involve all stakeholders who use the technology. Develop a formal evaluation process to assess each of the vendors that you investigate.

Selecting or changing your system

A telephone system is a critical component of your management information systems. Don't limit your assessment; your telephone system deserves the same level of scrutiny that you exercise when selecting a practice management or EHR system.

Complete these steps before selecting or changing your telephone system:

- Learn telephone system terms and procedures. Like the healthcare industry, the telecommunications market is full of acronyms and technical terminology. Familiarizing yourself with the nomenclature keeps you on equal footing with your potential vendors. Exhibit 6.3 lists common terms associated with telephone systems and a brief definition of each.

➤ Learn the basic telephone equipment structure. Knowing the system's parts and features improves the outcome of your system evaluation process.

➤ Define your practice's needs. Review your existing system, as well as the features of the potential new system. Do you want better reporting, an enhanced ability to route or transfer callers, or extra features like automatic call distribution? Identify the specific features needed for your practice.

[EXHIBIT 6.3] **Common features of telephone systems**

Automated (auto) attendant: A system that answers and routes calls after prompting callers. For example, "Thank you for calling Medical Practice Associates. If this is an emergency, please hang up and dial 9-1-1. Please press one of the following options so that we can best direct your call to meet your needs: press 1 to schedule or cancel an appointment; press 2 to renew a prescription; press 3 to request a test result; press 4 to speak with a nurse; press 5 to discuss your bill. Please press 0 for all other calls or to speak with an operator."

Automatic call distributor (ACD) or uniform call distributor (UCD): Software products that help telephone operators better manage incoming calls by distributing calls evenly to staff, pointing callers to specific functions (for example, appointment requests and prescription renewals), and placing callers on automatic hold – "in queue" – until a staff member is available to take the call. ACDs or UCDs can be used in place of or as a back-up for your receptionist.

Call accounting: Software programs that capture, record, analyze, and organize call data. The information is stored in a database that can be queried for operator productivity, call abandonment rate, and other analyses.

Call forwarding: A function that allows you to program the system to ring elsewhere if a station is busy or a call is not answered within a predetermined number of rings. Some systems permit external forwarding; some forward only within the system.

Call hunt: A function that bounces incoming calls automatically to the next available (not busy) line.

(continues)

> **[EXHIBIT 6.3]** **Common features of telephone systems (continued)**

Call park: A function that allows you to place callers "in orbit," removing them from general telephone traffic to alert staff that a call is waiting.

Call transfer: A function that allows calls received from internal or external callers to be sent from one telephone to any other within the system.

Caller identification (ID): A function that allows you to identify the caller's registered name and number.

Capacity: The number of telephones, lines, and software that a telephone system can handle. For example, a 24-port system can handle a combination of 24 lines and telephones.

Central processing unit (CPU): The main cabinet that houses the telephone system's intelligence and controls its activities.

Custom call routing (CCR): A function that enables you to design custom routing points for callers – a big plus offered by some auto attendants. For example, a caller can leave a message in a mailbox and then be routed to specific locations within a business.

Direct inward dialing (DID): A function that enables a caller to bypass the receptionist and be routed directly to the desired extension. DID trunks are assigned through the telephone company. Each trunk ordered has 24 associated telephones, each of which can be assigned to individual staff members.

Interactive voice response (IVR): Software that prompts callers for information by asking them to use their telephone keypads or, in some systems, utter certain phrases in response to automated questions. IVR improves staff efficiency by routing callers to the appropriate staff based on information the caller provides.

Intercom: A function that enables you to ring another telephone within the system and talk internally without tying up an outside line.

Port: A port is the point of connections in a system. Consider this the interface point at which programs are routed into the telephone system. A two-port voicemail system enables two activities; a four-port voicemail system allows four; an eight-port, eight. Ports are avenues that are open for travel when connected to a CPU.

(continues)

> **[EXHIBIT 6.3]** Common features of telephone systems (continued)

Predictive dialer: A system focused on managing *outbound* calls, this technology automatically dials batches of telephone numbers for connection to staff. Based on parameters established by management, these systems adjust the calling process to the number of staff members it anticipates (or predicts) will be available when the calls being placed are expected to be answered. The predictive dialer discards unanswered calls, engaged numbers, disconnected lines, answers from fax machines, voicemail and similar automated services, and only connects staff to the calls that are actually answered by people. This technology practically eliminates wasted staff time by connecting telephone operators with a live person immediately.

Remote notification: A pager or cellular phone notifies the user that he or she has a voicemail message.

T1: A digital transmission link with a capacity of 1.544 Mbps (1,544,000 bits of data per second). T1 normally can handle 24 simultaneous voice conversations or data links over two pairs of wires, each one digitized at 64 Kbps. This is accomplished by using special encoding and decoding equipment at each end of the transmission path to multiplex one circuit into 24 channels. The next generation of this technology, T2 and T3 lines, carries multiple T1 channels multiplexed, resulting in higher transmission rates (6.312 and 44.736 Mbps, respectively).

Telephony: The use or operation of an apparatus or device for the transmission of sounds between distinct, separate points (can be with or without connecting wires).

Traffic: The number of users on a call.

Trunk: A line or telephone number.

Voice over Internet protocol (VoIP): A technology that enables routing of voice conversations over the Internet or any other IP network. The voice data flows over a general-purpose packet-switched network instead of the traditional dedicated, circuit-switched voice transmission lines. Also referred to as IP telephony and Internet telephony.

Wireless telephone: A portable telephone that can fully integrate into your system and can be used from anywhere in your office.

- Involve your staff. Speaking with all of your staff members to discuss specific needs, functions, and ideas for functionality helps you choose the right system for your practice.
- Network with other practices of similar size and structure. Reach out to at least three colleagues to inquire about their systems – and the advantages and disadvantages of each.
- Gather information and proposals from vendors. Select three to five vendors to submit a request for proposal for your telephone system. The more specific you are, the more information you will garner from the proposals.
- Do your homework. Before you establish a relationship with the company that will manage your communications, investigate the vendors. Deal only with quality vendors. The telephone is your main communication portal to external customers (patients and referring physicians), as well as your internal network.
- Understand your patients. No matter what features or applications you consider, keep in mind the needs of your patient population. Pay special attention to the design of an automated system if large numbers of your patients are not used to dealing with automated telephones or English is not their primary language.

Analyze the investment

After the telephone system (or a new feature, enhancement, or software product) is installed, gauge where it works and does not work. Spend a few minutes each day in your reception area asking patients for their opinions. Obtain feedback from your key referring physicians and their staff. Be sure to solicit advice from the staff at your entire practice, as it affects everyone from the receptionist to the physicians, as well as your patients. Ask: Is it effective? Has it saved you time and/or money? Has it made your practice more efficient? Has it decreased or increased your response time to patients? Is your "return on investment" positive? If not, what steps can you take to improve the system?

Expect to use the system for at least six weeks before you see any impact on response times and costs. If the answers to the above questions are a resounding "no" for a particular feature, such as an ACD, then don't invest in an ACD and attendant, particularly if you can place your efforts into directing patients to communicate with you via online, secure electronic messaging, or an online patient portal instead.

Consider workflow

Map your practice's workflow to ensure that this new technology is used efficiently. Your callers, regardless of where or how the call is routed, should receive a timely response.

Choose with care

Carefully select the product and the vendor. Study the vendor's track record. Talk to several other practices that use the system. Negotiate a trial period to test the system, and don't skimp on service or training. Are all of these cautions really necessary? Yes! Your patients may never forgive you for losing their calls, and you may place your practice into a risk management situation.

 BEST PRACTICE

> Investigate telephony applications that integrate with your systems to place outbound calls to patients – such as appointment reminders – freeing up telephone staff for tasks that are knowledge intensive.

Telephony Applications

Telecommunications software products (referred to collectively as telephony applications) are now readily available for use in a medical practice. These software products integrate with your information systems to replicate or back up services that your practice currently provides. For example, you can purchase appointment confirmation systems that integrate with your practice management system (the scheduling module, in particular). These systems access the schedule for the following day and initiate calls and/or text messages to remind patients of their appointments. The software finds the telephone numbers associated with each patient's name and places outbound calls or texts to those numbers to communicate a reminder for the patient's upcoming appointment. Systems can be established to call only the patient's primary telephone number or they can work through the alternate telephone numbers the patient has provided for appointment reminders. In addition to appointment confirmations, telephony applications can assist practices with a multitude of functions, many of which are highlighted in Exhibit 6.4.

Other Considerations

In addition to the configuration of a system's key functions, there are a host of other factors to consider when selecting or implementing a telephone system. Evaluate the following issues as you refine your telephone system.

If your practice provides services that may be considered sensitive (such as psychiatry, obstetrics, oncology, and infectious disease), consider blocking your practice's "caller identification (ID)" when calling patients. Without blocking, your practice's name and number may appear on the recipient's caller ID display when you call patients to remind them of appointments or report that test results have arrived. This identification could compromise the patient's confidentiality if others in the household or business see it. Instead, consider using a number that remains unidentified, often displaying as "private caller" on recipients' telephones. Many practices have begun to use this feature to avoid patients automatically calling your number back (an almost instantaneous process on most cellular phones today, which creates a trail of all "missed calls"), before listening to your message or even when no message is left. Avoid a specific identification of one particular area of your practice – the business office – on your caller ID. If the name "business office" appears on your patients' cellular phones when one of your staff members calls, there's no guarantee that *any* patient will respond to your call.

While patients are waiting on hold or being transferred, use the opportunity to deliver custom messages about your practice. After being placed on hold, the patient is essentially captive. Avoid blank space or elevator music; instead, use on-hold messaging to communicate important information that provides value to your patients – and your practice. For example, record a message with an invitation to register for your online patient portal. Or use the opportunity to disseminate information regarding vaccine availability and flu shots. You can either focus on disseminating information about services you offer or supplement your message with answers to frequently asked questions. The best sources to discover these common questions are your staff and telephone logs (see Chapter 2). Key in on the subjects that produce the highest call volume where staff members are essentially repeating the same message over and over to callers. In addition to saving staff time, you may be able to reduce the number of future incoming calls requesting this information.

 BEST PRACTICE

> While patients are waiting on hold, use the opportunity to deliver custom messages about your practice, such as an invitation to register for your online patient portal.

> **[EXHIBIT 6.4]** Telephony applications
>
> - Appointment reminders and confirmations
> - Test results reporting
> - Collection calls
> - Patient educational material requests
> - Pre-recorded patient instructions and explanations
> - Prescription requests
> - Staff notifications
> - Patient satisfaction surveys

Summary

If you need to select a new telephone system or change the capabilities of your current system, use the same intense scrutiny as you would when selecting a practice management or EHR system. Deploy your best efforts to match a system's capability with your practice's telephone demand. Buying new equipment, by itself, isn't the sole answer to keeping telephone demand in check. Before shopping for new technology, examine your current processes to see where you can change telephone management or even reduce telephone demand. Then, by enhancing your operations and deploying technology, you can begin to help yourself – and your patients – to focus more of your days on improving health and less of it on answering telephones.

[CHAPTER 7]

Call Centers

Do you need a call center for your medical practice? In this chapter, we explore call centers and help you determine whether it is time to consolidate inbound telephones in your medical practice. Whether your practice is large or small, the development of a well-executed call center offers a unique opportunity to showcase the practice's attention to patient and referring physician satisfaction and successfully achieve the goals of improving patient access and service delivery. Recent healthcare trends place additional importance on an intentionally designed call center to efficiently handle a practice's communication.

In this chapter, you will learn the various aspects of a call center, which include:

- The definition of a call center;
- Key decision steps in call center formation;
- How to staff a call center;
- Workforce efficiency;
- Designing a call center; and
- Best practices in call center management.

What Is a Call Center?

A call center is a group of employees, typically co-located in the same physical space, who are focused on appropriately and efficiently handling the telephone calls of an organization. Alternative names that are being embraced by medical practices include "contact center" and "access center." Although telephone staff members have historically been referred to as "switchboard operators" or "agents," call center employees are increasingly being referred to as "patient navigators" and "access coordinators." These titles reflect the importance of the call center to the practice and its stakeholders.

The scope of a call center has no boundaries. There is no minimum number of staff members required to constitute a call center; it's not uncommon to have a call center staffed by three employees – or more than 40. There are no specifics on the size or specialty of the medical practice; practices with just a few physicians – or those with hundreds of physicians – can institute and operate a successful call center. Furthermore, there is no definition of the type of calls that the call center handles. In a medical practice, a center can focus on incoming telephone calls only, or a mixture of incoming and outgoing calls. Moreover, the call center may handle all calls – clinical, registration, insurance, and scheduling, as well as billing – or just one of these functions. Referring physicians may be the only callers routed to the call center, patients may be the sole focus, or calls managed by the call center may be a combination of both. Finally, the nature of the call center varies. A call center can serve as a switchboard operation using employees to distribute calls to the appropriate party or it can manage the full gamut of callers' needs – a "one call does it all" approach. Although the designation "call center" may be simple, the structure, composition, and staffing of the center are far from elementary.

Why begin the journey of exploring a call center for your practice? When patients or referring physicians call your practice, they expect to receive a consistent and standard experience; however, as various employees throughout the practice answer calls, this standard experience is difficult to implement and enforce. Practices can use various tools and scripts that target employees; however, enforcing consistency and providing the standard experience across numerous positions and extensions are difficult to achieve. A call center offers the opportunity to consolidate this initial contact within the practice, allowing one group of dedicated employees who have received focused training and reinforcement to handle calls with a consistent approach and experience for the caller. For a call center, success is typically measured via its ability to manage the volume at the expected level of quality. Although there are dozens of measurements associated with quality, the one most often used by call centers is service level. *Service level* is defined as the percentage of calls that are answered within a pre-defined wait threshold. (See Chapter 2 for a discussion of various quality measures associated with telephone operations, including service level.)

BEST PRACTICE

A call center offers the opportunity to consolidate the initial contact with the practice to a group of dedicated staff with focused training. Measure the quality of the call center by its service level. Service level is the percentage of calls that are answered within a pre-defined wait threshold.

Appropriately responding to the call is just the beginning. Many practices have staff members who have a large, diverse workload. For staff members who are tasked with serving the needs of physicians, nurses, and patients being seen in the office, picking up the telephone is not always a priority. Thus, the use of voicemail is very high in these scenarios, and response times to callers are often very poor. In sum, when telephones are under *everyone's* purview, they are often no one's responsibility.

In addition to dedicated staff, focused oversight and management can be beneficial. When calls are distributed to extensions throughout the practice, it is difficult to specify an individual who has primary responsibility for how the calls are handled and the service is delivered. Decentralized call models are often managed by leaders who are also charged with additional responsibilities for front office, revenue cycle functions, and clinical support, to name a few. In contrast, a call center offers direct oversight concentrated on managing communication with patients and/or referring physicians. This focused expertise is critical in managing telephone-based interactions that are not as controlled as patient arrivals at a front office. As every practice knows, calls do not come into the queue consistently throughout the day; they can be sporadic and difficult to predict, and the reasons for inbound calls are diverse. The potential to successfully and cost-effectively allocate and manage staff resources while maintaining superior levels of quality is what a dedicated call center can deliver.

In this chapter, we focus primarily on responding and processing telephone calls; however, in today's environment, a call center is no longer limited to focusing on communicating via the telephone. Communication methods now include e-mail, electronic messaging, chat, and social media, all of which need to be considered when developing the communication approach of the practice and the potential role of the call center in managing these new methods. Be aware that regulatory issues can arise with handling these other types of communication.

Key Decision Steps in Call Center Development

As part of your overall communications strategy and to gain a better understanding of the discussion that follows, let's explore some key considerations to determine if a call center is the right solution for your medical practice.

Current quality

First, assess your current level of quality related to your response time and handling of telephones. Use the tools in Chapter 2 to measure your telephones and compare your current state with your service expectations. Determine your ability to process calls by measuring the percentage of calls you handle within a certain time period (for example, 80 percent within 30 seconds). In addition, analyze your abandonment rate. Not only does a high rate represent a service improvement opportunity, but it may signal a risk management issue as well. In addition to measuring these data and others regarding the quality of your telephone operations as derived from your telephone system, consider querying your callers. That is, ask patients and referring physicians for feedback regarding your telephone operations. Hearing the "voice of the customer" is often the ideal way to determine if it is the right time to embark on a call center for your practice. The voice of the customer can also help to convince internal stakeholders that a change is needed. If your current performance falls below your expectations – or those of your callers – consider a call center to provide improved focus and service to telephone management.

Current staffing levels

Second, evaluate your current staffing levels and compare them to staffing workload ranges, as demonstrated in Chapter 4. If your telephones are over- or understaffed, whether that task is focused or just one of many jobs for an employee, it may be time to consider a consolidated unit to manage your telephones. The training costs and time required to educate new staff regarding telephone management may be repetitive for your practice. A central unit is able to mitigate the service variation due to staff turnover, absences, or departures by having a central, core team focused on the telephones.

Reasons for inbound calls

As a third step in the assessment process for a call center, evaluate the reasons for inbound telephone calls to your practice. Use the tools in Chapter 2 to obtain the reasons for inbound calls to your practice. Exhibit 7.1 highlights key functions often served by a call center, but there is no need to be constrained in your approach. A call center may receive calls from referring physicians as well as calls from patients related to scheduling, triage and advice, general information requests, medical records requests, prescription renewals, and test results. By assessing the reasons for inbound calls, you are in a position to determine if call consolidation makes sense for your practice.

Delegated authority to manage calls

Next, identify the optimal action you would want call center staff to take when responding to the inbound telephone calls if you had a call center. As depicted in Exhibit 7.2, for example, the action for a physician-to-physician call for this medical practice is for call center staff to have the knowledge and tools to either connect the physicians directly or send the referring physician to the on-call physician. As another example from Exhibit 7.2, if a patient calls to schedule or change an appointment, the practice would want its call center staff to be able to make or change an appointment directly, not simply transfer the caller to a scheduler. Evaluate the reasons for your inbound calls and determine the delegated authority you would want to provide to the call center.

[CHAPTER 7] | CALL CENTERS

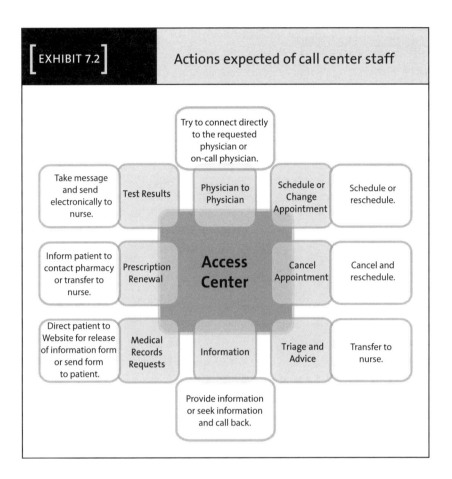

Exhibit 7.2: Actions expected of call center staff

BEST PRACTICE

To determine if a call center will benefit your practice, evaluate the current quality of your telephones and the current staffing levels to ascertain the magnitude of improvement opportunity. Then outline the delegated authority you would want to provide to the call center staff to manage the key reasons for inbound calls. This will help you assess the need for a consolidated call center operation.

If your medical practice determines that the call center must transfer all scheduling calls to a scheduling unit or the physician's nurse, then perhaps a central call center would not be effective in your practice. It may serve as only another step or barrier for patients who simply want to make an appointment to see you. But if many of the calls can be handled by call center staff as opposed to being redirected to practice staff, then a call center can provide economies of scale for telephone work. The practice can also benefit from consolidating the knowledge and expertise needed to effectively manage inbound call demand.

A call center offers great potential to add specific strategies that improve both practice efficiency and the overall patient experience. If the transition to a call center is well planned with intentionally designed processes, the structure of a call center offers advantages that cannot be achieved by other systems.

Staffing a Call Center

Since staffing is often one of the key considerations in implementing a consolidated center, let's explore how to staff a call center and the impact of quality related to staffing. As discussed previously, call centers have the potential to provide a more consistent level of quality to patients by allowing the practice to dedicate a specific structure to prioritize the telephones and provide oversight by management. All of these benefits can be eroded if the call center does not have – and maintain – an appropriate number of employees. The quantity of inbound calls, as well as the quality of telephone management, must be constantly analyzed.

As demonstrated in Exhibit 7.3, a call center can falter if staffing levels are not appropriate. In this example, let's assume that the call center employs 10 staff members with approximately 12,000 calls per month, but two employees decide to leave. Staff attrition impacts quality quickly. Quality, as measured by service level in this example,

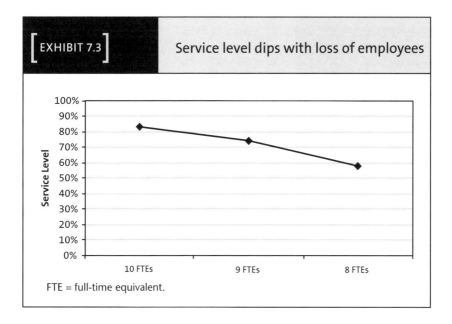

falls from an acceptable 82 percent of calls answered within 30 seconds to less than 60 percent with the loss of the two staff members.

In addition to staff fluctuations, a key management issue for call centers is to evaluate and handle the variation of incoming calls. There is no appointment schedule for telephone calls; inbound calls are scattered throughout the day and the week. Call centers are challenged to predict these fluctuations and address the impact in a cost-effective manner.

Exhibit 7.4 highlights the fluctuation in volume by day of the week in one practice. Calls also fluctuate by time of day, further complicating a staffing model as demonstrated in Exhibit 7.5.

If all patient calls are equally important – whether they arrive Monday, Wednesday, or Friday, or at 8 a.m. or noon – then the goal is to ensure consistently positive service throughout the week, as well as the day. Without a clear staffing strategy, call centers don't have enough employees to handle peak volumes, which causes quality to

[EXHIBIT 7.4] Weekly inbound call demand by day of week

[EXHIBIT 7.5] Inbound call demand by time of day

plunge, or they have too many employees, which is expensive and may leave an excess of non-value-added downtime.

Forecasting call volumes

To mitigate problems from inappropriate staffing, it's important to develop a formal staffing model for your call center. At minimum, you need to acknowledge the call volumes you expect. This is always an interesting exercise that combines both science and art as you attempt to predict future volumes based on information from the past. Fortunately, there are several call models to explore that help align your specific volumes with the staff needed to meet a targeted level of quality. In this section, we present three models – from very basic to sophisticated – to consider when factoring your practice's staffing needs.

BEST PRACTICE

> To determine the appropriate staffing model for your call center, use basic forecasting, the Erlang C method, and/or workforce management tools. The goal is to develop a staffing model aligned with both call volumes and quality expectations.

Basic forecast

A nontechnical method can be used to produce a rudimentary forecast model for staffing a call center. The following three items are needed to calculate this model. This model is similar to the staffing example we provided in Chapter 4. Although it would be ideal to measure this over a significant period of time, we recommend an evaluation time frame of one month.

1. **Call volume:** The volume of calls by day of week and time of day can usually be obtained from the telephone system. This provides basic data to understand the volume of inbound calls to the practice. (For example, 75 calls are received by the practice on Mondays between 8 a.m. and 9 a.m.)
2. **Call type:** Ask staff members who manage your primary telephone extension to use manual tick-mark sheets to provide a rough breakdown of the types of calls received by the practice. This allows you to estimate how many calls are strictly for scheduling, clinical callbacks, prescription renewal requests, and so forth.
3. **Average duration:** Finally, determine the average call duration, which is referred to as "talk time" for telephone operations, associated with each type of call. For example, your average scheduling call may consume 4.5 minutes.

Focusing on the examples presented above, let's assume the practice receives 38 calls related to scheduling on Monday morning between 8 a.m. and 9 a.m. Each scheduling call takes an average of 4.5 minutes to complete; therefore, the total minutes needed during this hour to answer these calls is 171 minutes of work. Dividing that time by the 60 minutes that constitutes an hour, 2.85 FTEs (full-time equivalents) are required. You would need to repeat this calculation for each call type and hour of day to arrive at your overall hourly staffing plan, keeping in mind that this basic calculation does not account for employee downtime or the variation in call arrival. Because it is limited to data regarding call volume and duration, the model does not take quality into consideration. Therefore, if this staffing model is embraced, we recommend that the staff estimates be rounded upward. The 2.85 FTEs in this example should be translated into 3.00 FTEs. After staff members have been assigned, quality must be monitored carefully to ensure that the number of employees who have been deployed are adequate, as it is not uncommon for this model to underestimate the staff required to maintain a base of satisfied callers.

Erlang C method

The second method to staff a call center is one of the most widely used models today for forecasting call center staffing levels. It derives its name from A.K. Erlang, a Danish engineer who developed the original queuing and trafficking theory. The equation that formulates the method dubbed Erlang C, which is presented below, accounts for volume and duration, as well as quality.

$$P_W = \frac{\frac{A^N}{N!} \frac{N}{N-A}}{\sum_{i=0}^{N-1} \frac{A^i}{i!} + \frac{A^N}{N!} \frac{N}{N-A}}$$

where:

➤ P_w is the probability that a customer has to wait for service

➤ A is the total traffic offered in units of erlangs

➤ N is the number of servers

We could spend the next chapter going through what each letter and symbol means, as well as how to use this formula. Don't worry; we won't launch into a detailed explanation. Instead, we recommend that you use an Internet search engine to query "Erlang C." In your search, you will uncover a list of Websites that offer an Erlang C calculator where you can enter key data as inputs and the formula is automatically calculated for you. Expect to enter call volume and duration. The third input is the desired service level. Changing the service level alters the output, which is the number of employees needed to handle the call volume and call duration at the desired service level.

There are two key assumptions to be aware of when using the Erlang C method:

1. Erlang C assumes that the rate of calls is consistent over the defined period, which results in the inability of the model to account for the impact of the variation of call arrivals often experienced with a call center.

2. Erlang C assumes that calls unable to reach a live operator remain in the queue until answered; calls are not abandoned or blocked by the system. Thus, the model does not account for caller behavior.

Despite these drawbacks, Erlang C is still a very useful (and free!) tool in determining staffing needs, as it is readily available and simple to use.

Workforce management tools

The third method for staffing a call center involves workforce management tools. Several vendors in the call center market offer workforce management tools as a stand-alone program or a package coupled with other features. These are very powerful tools because they calculate staffing needs based on a detailed history of calls, including call volume, duration, staff downtime, call arrival patterns, and caller behavior (such as tolerance for hold times before abandoning the call). Using all of this data, often extracted directly from the telephone system (without the need to monitor, analyze, or input information), a workforce management tool can offer a very accurate snapshot of staff needed by time of day and day of week based on the desired level of quality. See Exhibit 7.6 for a sample hourly forecast of staff based on a workforce management tool.

Workforce Efficiency

Determining the number of staff needed at different intervals throughout the day and week is the first step in designing a staffing strategy for a call center. How those resources are applied becomes crucial in maximizing efficiency. Let's review some of the key strategies to apply; some of which can be used by all practices, even in the absence of a call center.

BEST PRACTICE

Employ part-time staff to meet service-level expectations. This permits a call center to maintain a consistent, high level of quality throughout the day at a fraction of the cost.

Part-time staffing

Part-time employees are a vital asset for telephone operations. Look for parts of the day or week that part-time staff members can be applied to target their efforts and to avoid reductions in the quality of your telephone management. For example, a call center may be able to maintain the level of quality that meets the practice's expectations for most of the day; however, when employees begin taking lunch, even though they are staggered over several hours, poor performance may ensue. See Exhibit 7.7 for a display of data, including the area identified as "Opportunity." As this exhibit demonstrates,

[EXHIBIT 7.7] Opportunity identified: part-time staff can be the solution

incorporating a 10 a.m. to 2 p.m. shift of part-time staff into the practice's call center would greatly improve the overall performance of the calls being handled. Incorporating part-time staff into your strategy essentially allows the practice to eliminate the decline in quality by effectively addressing the problem segment of the day at a fraction of the cost of a full-time employee.

The 10 a.m. to 2 p.m. time frame is an advantageous target because there are typically excellent candidates available to apply for the position. Because of the hours, this opportunity often attracts candidates interested in part-time positions that can accommodate their time with school-aged children. This time period targets the practice's major need, as staffing is usually reduced during this time and call volumes during this period are often high. An alternative solution to part-time staffing is to hire a vendor to take calls after a certain service level is reached, thereby supplementing the call center staffing to ensure quality performance.

BEST PRACTICE

Establish first-call resolution as a goal and deploy strategies to make this goal a reality for your telephone operation.

First-call resolution

First-call resolution, a concept discussed in Chapter 5, is the goal for most call centers. Effectively routing the call to the best resource with the knowledge and skill to manage the call is the key to achieving this goal. Since patients call a practice for various needs, the ability to achieve this routing efficiently and effectively can be a challenge. Although there is no single right answer, the following describes four popular options to address first-call resolution:

1. Train staff members to handle the vast majority of calls received by the call center. These must be highly skilled operators who are trained to handle myriad issues.

2. Deploy a small group of staff members who act as call distributors. These operators answer the call and then quickly distribute these calls to the appropriate party—nurses, schedulers, billers, and so forth.

3. Use an automatic call distributor (ACD) that puts the onus on the patient to choose the resource. Through the system, route the call to the appropriate staff member to handle the caller's needs.

4. Create a series of multiple telephone numbers or extensions that allow callers to be seamlessly routed to the appropriate staff member, all of whom may be co-located within the same call center.

Evaluate the solution that is best for your practice, based on your telephone system and staff resources, as well as your expectations for call management and quality.

Best agent routing

As you consider how calls are organized, it is important to determine *who* can best handle the callers' needs. To achieve the goals of a call center – first-call resolution, as well as the desired level of quality – the concept of "best agent routing" is an important consideration. Best agent routing allows the caller to be routed to the staff member who is best qualified to meet his or her needs. This concept is particularly essential for new staff members who may have been assigned to process a particular type of call but need more time and/or training to handle the call. For a staff member assigned to appointment scheduling, for example, a model may be deployed to route calls from established patients to operators who have one year's experience or less, while more seasoned staff members handle new patient calls. By using best agent routing and ramping up the employee over time, the call center experiences higher first-call resolution and lower hold times. This system also increases first-year satisfaction of the call center by decreasing the learning curve frustration. Although best agent routing is not always possible, discuss the concept with your telephone system vendor to work together to determine how callers can best be routed.

 BEST PRACTICE

Adopt best agent routing to link the caller to the staff member best qualified to meet the caller's needs. This helps the call center to have higher first-call resolution and it lowers hold times.

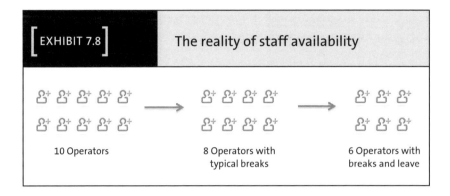

Staff availability

One of the key challenges in handling telephone operations within a call center is to resolve the inevitable fluctuations in staff availability without a noticeable variation in service to the patient. As noted in the previous staff analysis, 171 minutes dictated the need for 2.85 FTEs. However, the reality is that 2.85 FTEs is not actually 171 minutes. Staff members can't handle calls while they are getting a cup of coffee from the break room, using the rest room, receiving training on the new telephone system, or meeting with you to discuss their performance. Indeed, all of these activities result in time away from the telephones. Accounting for standard breaks, the most efficient state of a call center employee is 85 percent productive. Adding in vacation, sickness, and turnover, this can rapidly fall to 60 percent, quickly changing what appears to be a well-staffed call center into a poor-performing one! (See Exhibit 7.8.)

> The most efficient state of a call center employee is for the employee to be 85 percent productive. Make sure your call center staff meets this productivity threshold.

Call centers need to keep such fluctuations in mind and staff accordingly. Staffing options include:

- Overstaff all telephone positions to ensure that downtime is covered;
- Employ part-time staff targeted during predictable periods of high call volumes and/or planned absences to minimize any negative impact;
- Use either an external or internal temporary staffing pool to help cover times of need; and
- Cross-train practice staff (for example, a medical assistant) to provide temporary telephone coverage.

Because overstaffing – sinking a significant amount of expenses into the call center – is not a realistic option, the practice must consider the best method to deploy additional staff as needed.

As discussed earlier in this chapter, best agent routing is a method of grouping the complexity of calls so that the easiest calls can be specifically routed to a staff member or group of employees. With best agent routing, temporary staff, or perhaps even staff members at the practice who are available but typically assigned to other tasks can be assigned to handle the least complex calls. This model allows the call center to manage the call volume at the desired level of quality – at the lowest cost possible.

Call leveling

It is intuitive that there is a variation in the arrival of calls to a medical practice. This fluctuation in volume results in time periods in which there are only a few inbound calls – and moments when the telephone lines are flooded. These times of heavy call volumes are often referred to as call spikes. Call spikes can cause practices to invest in staff to manage them (who then sit idle during periods of low volume) – or result in low performance in terms of meeting callers' expectations regarding quality. Deploying a strategy to minimize the impact of call spikes on your practice helps to reduce staff costs and improve performance. Focus on "call leveling," also referred to as call shifting – a tactic that features looking for opportunities that transfer workload to times of predictably lower volume.

BEST PRACTICE

Adopt call leveling, such as a virtual hold system, to look for opportunities to transfer work to times of predictably lower volume.

Although it may seem impossible to influence the arrival rate of calls, there are opportunities to shift calls. On the ACD, program an alternative route that is revealed if the hold time exceeds two minutes (or another time period that you determine is best for your callers). This option allows a patient to opt into voicemail and receive a return call within the hour rather than continue to wait on hold. A similar alternative is to use a "virtual hold" system. This system is best applied to call centers experiencing heavy call volumes with extended waits in the queue. Patients are provided the option of exiting out of the call but remaining in a virtual queue until the call is ready to be handled. When the calls that previously arrived are cleared, the system automatically calls back the patient who is next in line. This is a very useful tool to remove callers' frustration when they are holding in the queue for the next available operator.

For calls with a significant hold time, consider shifting these "overflow" calls to a vendor to answer the call with a live voice and provide the caller with an option to remain in the queue or leave a message for callback. This gives the patient an option if call waits increase. Although all overflow calls can be sent to an external vendor, protocols can be established based on ACD options. For example, clinical calls could be sent to a vendor specializing in nurse triage. The vendor can either resolve the patient's needs or complete a message and transmit it to the internal nursing team for follow-up. Another example is travel directions. These calls are usually time-consuming and most vendors can field these well, or the patient could be directed to a pre-recorded travel directions message. As discussed in detail in Chapter 3, reducing the demand for calls by offering alternative communication routes (for example, online patient portal or personal health record for medication renewals, appointment requests, and clinical messaging) is the ideal method of call leveling.

Automated appointment scheduling protocols

The task of scheduling appointments for established and new patients is often delegated to the call center in a medical practice. Because the schedule represents the essence of a practice, effectively managing the scheduling process is essential. For many practices, scheduling protocols are recorded in large three-ring binders or on a series of sticky notes that landscape the cubicles of staff members. Not only is it difficult to manage the information in such a format, it is almost always out of date. Automating the scheduling logic is an important factor in reducing the complexity of provider scheduling – and aiding the call center tasked with managing it.

 BEST PRACTICE

> Create a knowledge center. For example, automate the scheduling logic and develop a series of questions and scripts to help call center staff link patients to the appropriate provider.

Develop an electronic version of the appointment scheduling protocols to serve as a readily accessible, easily updatable knowledge center. Using the binders and notes to build the reference, create a tool that presents staff with a series of questions and scripts that end with the appropriate physician or provider, as well as the visit type.

Give staff dual monitors, with the practice's practice management system on one monitor and the knowledge center on the other. Your practice may have the internal expertise to develop such a tool itself; if not, vendors can assist you in creating these protocols. Update the tool regularly to remain accurate. In addition to improving scheduling accuracy, which leads to enhanced revenue, the tool can serve as a resource for new staff members who are learning scheduling protocols. Of course, the knowledge center can be extended beyond scheduling protocols, to include various aspects of the practice's operations that may be useful to all staff and providers.

Quality and training

Most of the strategies we discuss in this chapter are focused on the timeliness of call center staff in answering the telephones. However, once answered, the *quality* of the call is the determining factor driving satisfaction.

If you develop a call center for your medical practice, institute a quality program focused on adherence to the quality indicators we first described in Chapter 2 – including scripting, appropriate tone, call resolution, accuracy, and first-call resolution. To successfully measure performance, the quality program must feature an evaluation of actual calls. Thus, the telephone system must be able to record calls and, ideally, identify them by operator. This technology can be purchased as a stand-alone product or packaged with other software. The ability to capture and monitor call recordings is essential. When staff members are asked to listen to their interactions with patients after the call has been completed, it is often a very different experience than what they are able to recall.

Although there is no pre-determined volume of calls that must be reviewed, consider a minimum of 10 per staff member per year for a performance evaluation. (Additional call reviews at a more frequent period are recommended, but resource availability must be considered.) Monitored calls should be reviewed with staff members on a timely and consistent basis so that employees can learn from their telephone interactions. Use both positive calls and calls where the staff member has an opportunity for improvement when sharing the calls with staff for performance assessment and improvement.

Call recordings are arguably the best tool for quieting naysayers of the call center, if applicable. By recording 100 percent of calls, the manager of the call center is able to respond to any complaints about service, scheduling errors, or protocols that were perceived not to be followed.

The quality program can be managed and conducted centrally or, for a large operation, decentralized to local supervisory management. The benefits of a central quality program can include unbiased call ratings, as opposed to local management who may instill personal bias in the ratings of the calls. Also, central quality monitoring offers consistent scoring that is difficult to achieve in a decentralized environment. If the program is decentralized, calibrate quality with reviewers to ensure that quality scores are comparative across managers.

To ensure success, couple the quality program with a comprehensive training program. Centralized and consistent training is a key benefit to the call center. When employees are trained together and work alongside one another, they can rely on each other to reinforce the training without adapting other practices. Training can be conducted in waves during business hours or it can include all staff members in training after business hours. If the training is focusing on a new process or tackling cultural competency issues, for example, after-hours training is preferred so that the group can learn and interact together. If training focuses on processes or is related to specific tasks, then a wave approach can work well. A well-rounded training program not only engages with staff members on or near their hire date, but also offers ongoing and consistent training throughout their careers.

BEST PRACTICE

Institute patient advisors into the call center training program to share their interactions with the call center and to help staff develop empathy and other skills to improve their performance.

Although there are many areas to be covered in a training program, a session dedicated to *empathy* is essential. Staff members are handling a multitude of calls back to back; it is very easy to forget who is on the other end of the telephone. Reinforce with staff that every call represents a patient, and one who is often struggling with serious medical problems. Recognizing and empathizing with the caller can help eliminate the belief that the calls being processed are of a routine nature. Since call centers no longer have face-to-face patient interactions, consider instituting "patient advisors" into the training plan. Patient advisors can be introduced in training sessions to provide actual examples of failing to meet performance expectations, lack of empathy, and so forth. Instead of just talking about the importance of the patient related to telephone operations, these patients can provide feedback directly to staff. These patient advisors consist of patients within your practice who are willing and interested in dedicating time for improvement efforts. Often, patients are eager to help the practice and can be a valuable resource in improving empathy among the staff. In addition, framing personal stories and pictures of patients within the call center reinforces the importance of displaying empathy in every telephone interaction.

BEST PRACTICE

Framing personal stories and pictures of patients within a call center reinforces the importance of displaying empathy in every telephone interaction.

[EXHIBIT 7.9] Three-step promotional path within a call center

Training initiatives should not just focus on staff within the call center. A practice's successful communication strategy impacts all staff throughout the practice, including providers and nursing staff. Include providers and staff in your development and training processes to identify call hand-off issues or integration opportunities before they negatively affect the performance of the telephone operations.

Career path

A perception exists that the career of a call center employee is limited to answering calls without any real opportunity for growth. Instituting multiple levels of job titles within the call center offers a promotional platform for those staff members that excel. Since call centers often handle more than incoming calls, and incoming calls can vary greatly in complexity, a promotional career path can be a win-win for employee and employer. Exhibit 7.9 provides an example of an approach that offers a three-step promotional path within the call center. This provides growth options for staff, rewards top performers within the center, and can minimize turnover.

Call Center Design

If a call center structure appears to be the right choice for your medical practice, let's cover some key considerations when moving from your practice's current state to the design of the new center.

Focused planning

Spending an appropriate time on the front end of the project by intentionally designing all aspects of the new center pays off with a quicker and less complicated implementation. Always keep the seamless integration of the patient, call center, and medical practice as the beacon of your design process. All decision points need to be compared back to the patient and referring physician experience.

Practice integration

Regardless of the type of call center you decide to build, integration within the practice is critical in delivering high-quality patient care. The call center and the practice must work as a team to resolve the needs of patients and referring physicians. If the call center does not act as the front line for the practice and effectively determine the best avenue for resolution, the practice will be hampered in its ability to deliver high-quality care. If the practice does not respond to the call center, patients are stuck in the middle trying to resolve their own needs. Both must work together in unison for the patient.

To ensure a successful integration, consider developing a "service level agreement" for both parties – the call center and the practice. This agreement should include the quality (for example, service level and abandonment rate) that is expected to be met or exceeded, the types of calls to be processed by the call center, and the general workflow of messaging as well as live calls. For the practice, the agreement should include a confirmation regarding the general workflow of messages and live calls, as well as the expected response time for live calls that are transferred and messages that are taken.

If a nurse doesn't respond to a message in the time frame communicated to the patient, for example, the patient will call again only to be greeted by a telephone operator who will have difficulty in managing the now-frustrated caller. Both parties should also agree to the process by which urgent or emergent calls are escalated, recognizing that the definition of "urgent" and "emergent" are in the hands of the patient or referring physician, not an internal debate between the practice and the call center. By placing workflow and expectations in writing, the practice can avoid challenges regarding the integration of its call center.

BEST PRACTICE

Develop a service level agreement that outlines the service expectations of the call center and the practice. Ensure that the call center meets established quality thresholds and the practice meets callback timelines.

Call types

A study regarding the types of inbound calls and their volume should be completed before a call center is launched. Determine how each type of call will be handled: Will all calls be handled by the call center? Will the call center route calls to another group? Will an ACD be implemented so that certain call types are directly routed to specific groups? Who are the "groups" who will handle the calls? How will the call center interact with them? Don't just launch a call center to start answering the telephone; develop a detailed process mapping of how all calls will be handled.

As a part of your study, be sure to measure the number of repeat calls. Repeat calls are not only an indication of inefficiency within the practice, but they will also drive up call center costs. Not only is your call center having to take an additional call, but a repeat call can double the average handle time as the patient is frustrated and items related to the call must receive immediate attention.

(See Chapter 2 for a detailed discussion regarding measuring telephone calls.)

Location

The location of the call center influences the level of attention that is paid to maintaining a cohesive team within the practice. If a call center is located off-site (which could mean across the street), the battle to avoid the "us against them" mentality must begin immediately. Off-site call centers need a plan that includes periodic face-to-face meetings between call center staff and the team at the practice. Attempt to conduct meetings outside of business hours so that call center employees can attend and be involved in the team. These meetings should occur at least quarterly to foster continued communication. Ensure that an agenda item within each meeting specifically addresses the call center/practice integration and communication. If you can't conduct after-hours meetings that everyone can attend, identify a rotating staff member who is assigned to attend meetings at the practice and be the representative for the call center. It is his or her responsibility to share call-center-related items with practice staff and also disseminate information back at the call center. Using a protocol to rotate the call center representative allows everyone the opportunity to integrate with the practice.

If open dialogue from the practice is not well planned, scheduling errors and other such miscommunications can inundate the call center and prevent it from focusing on performance improvement initiatives. When providers perceive that a call center employee cannot accurately schedule their patients, for example, mistrust ensues. To foster open communication, develop and promote the use of a simple form to facilitate feedback from providers and staff. The feedback form, preferably electronic, should be formulated in a manner such that a physician, provider, nurse, or other staff member can quickly complete and transmit it to the call center. The form should include the patient's name, date of birth, and any other qualifiers needed to identify the patient along with the error (reported by the caller or perceived to have occurred). When feedback is received, the call center must have an established process to research and provide timely resolution back to the physician, provider, nurse, or other staff member with any action steps taken. The ability to pull recorded calls and investigate the conversation, as discussed previously, is paramount in determining the cause of the complaint. Otherwise, call centers will always be managing within a "he said/she said" environment. Once researched, provide a timely response and be specific about the cause of the complaint. If the problem was a scheduling error on the staff member's part, for example, provide specifics about what actions will be taken to ensure that this does not happen again.

Stakeholders

Migrating the operations of the primary communication vehicle in a practice – the telephones – results in changes for all stakeholders. In addition to the changes that patients and referring physicians will experience, internal stakeholders – to include staff, practice administration, and providers – will undergo change. Treat the conversion to a new communication model as an opportunity for improvement, not as a detriment. During the transition from a model consisting of decentralized telephone operations to one that features a call center model, timely communication to all parties involved is crucial. Every stakeholder has a different opinion, and effort must be taken to manage their perceptions while the reality is being altered. Displaying a constant effort toward process improvement and transparency enables the practice to build the trust of stakeholders.

> **Staff.** If your practice pursues the development of a call center, make sure employees know what to expect, as they will be concerned not only about the changes involved in the transition but also the prospect of job losses. Involve an optimistic employee who has the respect of his or her peers in the design process of the call center. Publicly acknowledge the staff

member and commend the employee for his or her effort and insightful vision. This recognition keeps the team member on task and motivated. If another successful call center is located in close proximity to your practice, plan a site visit for your staff. Even if the call center is not in the healthcare industry, the visit aids management and employees in understanding the call center initiative. (Indeed, visiting a call center outside of the industry is a great idea to really engage staff in performance improvement; they see new ideas and methods that can be imported.) A site visit can demonstrate how a well-operated call center can be successful for all parties.

➤ **Administration.** It is not uncommon for practice leaders to carry a negative connotation because of personal experiences or anecdotes from other poorly executed call centers. It is important for the administration to recognize and embrace the benefits of a call center for the practice and, most importantly, the patients' experience. Practice leaders must publicly support the transition with physicians, providers, nurses, staff, and referring physicians' offices. Moreover, they must be able to articulate the vision of the call center. The administration must help set realistic expectations; it is typical to experience a slight degrading of performance during the transition. New processes need to be ironed out, and staff requires time to adjust to the new protocols and associated expectations. Ensure that all stakeholders understand that some pitfalls are expected in the transition so you can work to resolve any issues instead of concentrating on damage control with leadership.

➤ **Clinicians.** Physicians and other clinicians, as well as their clinical staff, might have numerous reasons why they believe a call center will not work. Including clinicians throughout the decision and design process is vital. Develop a timely, comprehensive communication plan for providers to ensure that they understand what the practice is trying to achieve. Include illustrations regarding the expected return on investment in terms of patient and referring physician satisfaction, increased appointments, and reduced abandonment rates. Recognize that the most common pushback from clinicians is: "my practice is too complex for a call center to manage."

Don't just start by employing new staff to answer and handle calls. Prior to implementing a call center, review and understand operations and workflow of the practice, to include the scheduling protocols of all physicians and providers. If current scheduling protocols require a doctorate to schedule the patient accurately, then effort must be made to simplify and streamline schedules. The knowledge center we discussed previously is a great tool to foster simplified scheduling protocols.

Perhaps the best information to present is feedback from patients and referring physicians who – if the practice takes the time to listen – are likely to share frustration regarding the practice's current telephone system. Instill in all stakeholders that a successful call center is an investment, not a cost. When effectively operated, a call center is an essential driver of profits throughout the practice.

 BEST PRACTICE

A successful call center is an investment, not a cost. When effectively operated, a call center is an essential driver of practice profits.

Summary

A call center can be an effective model to improve the communications of a practice, as well as patient access and service. To be successful, take the time to evaluate your current operations, as well as the design of a call center.

Concluding Remarks

The telephones have long been a source of frustration for many medical practices – and their patients. Use this book as a blueprint to measure, manage, and staff your telephones for optimal performance. Embrace the tools in this book, including telephone scripts, message-taking, callbacks, and telephony tools to help your staff members become experts in telephone management. The telephones are currently the primary access point to your medical practice. Make sure your telephones are staffed and managed with the diligence needed to optimize patient access and provide high-quality service to your patients.

It's your call: Master the telephones in your medical practice.

[APPENDIX]

Telephone Best Practices

This appendix summarizes the best practices we have cited throughout this book. Use this as a quick reference tool as you redesign your telephones for optimal performance.

Measure your key telephone performance measures – both volume and quality – to determine patient access opportunities for your medical practice.

You need to achieve the right balance of volume and quality to optimize telephone management.

Track the volume of repeat calls to your practice. A high volume of repeat calls is a signal that your practice can improve telephone operations and provide more timely patient access. Identifying and reducing repeat calls translate into higher patient satisfaction and less work for the practice.

If the percentages of outbound calls by topic match up with those of inbound calls, look for a better way to manage that type of call by leveraging technology and streamlining communication.

Call volume is typically four to five times the number of patient visits per day.... We believe that the call volume should be twice the number of patient visits, a goal achieved by practices that are successful at managing their telephones, reengineering their work processes, and deploying technology to enhance patient communication.

Make sure your callers receive a consistent call-handling experience. Patients will perceive the quality of your medical practice based on their service experience with your telephone staff.

There is no better way to obtain patient feedback than to ask your patients directly about their experience with your telephone staff. Make it part of your workday to sit down with patients in the reception area and ask probing questions about their perception of your practice.

Use a mystery patient telephone survey to learn whether telephone management is optimized for your practice.

Don't always rely on your own impressions; let the voice of the customer speak loud and clear.

What are your expectations for the telephones? Compare your current performance with your expectations and perform a gap analysis.

Don't just add more staff or upgrade your telephone system. Redesign your processes to improve telephone service, convert an inbound call to an outbound call, resolve the patient's needs on the first call, and strive to reduce overall inbound call demand.

Engage staff and physicians in reviewing telephone data and developing action plans to redesign key work processes to reduce telephone demand.

Ask the patient up front: "Do you want to be seen?" Turn nurse triage calls into patient visits.

Evaluate the percentage of your patients who end up rescheduling, cancelling, or not showing up. Consider changing your scheduling template time line if the percentage is greater than 5 percent.

The key is to control the process rather than let the process control you.

Give patients a portable tablet in the reception area for them to document questions for the physician and identify their current medications.

The better educated your patients are, the more efficient your medical practice can operate.

Implement "planned care visits" – proactively review patients' records before they present. For patients returning for a follow-up visit, evaluate expected documentation for imaging, lab, and consultant visits to which the patient was referred at the prior visit. Anticipate patients' needs by determining and outlining recommended care to address with the patient during the visit.

Videotape yourself communicating instructions to a patient, and post it on YouTube®.

If you want patients, as well as their family members and caregivers, to remember verbal instructions and information, give them a notepad and pen with which to write it down; encourage them to make notes on their iPad® or other portable device; or give them the information in writing.

Answer your telephones starting a minimum of 30 minutes before your office hours begin, and keep your telephones open at lunch.

Outbound telephone calls are more efficient because you're in control of the work; an inbound call controls you.

Do the work and do the work right the first time.

Make a virtual encounter part of each physician's day to attend to telephone messages, thereby ensuring a quick turnaround time to the caller – and avoiding repeat calls to the medical practice.

Before a message is taken, the operator should inquire of the caller: "Is there anything that I can do to help you?"

Staff your telephones with employees who have the requisite knowledge to help the caller, thereby eliminating the inefficiencies associated with "pass the caller."

Your telephone operator represents the patient's first impression of your practice. Make sure the employee has the knowledge and skills to manage a high volume of calls with quality and compassion.

Having the right staff starts with hiring the right staff.

Many medical practices have elected to hire staff with excellent customer service backgrounds and then train for medical terminology and medical practice operations.

Use social media to identify candidates and to evaluate the candidate's fit with your medical practice.

To determine the number of staff members you need to manage your telephones, use staff workload ranges. Be sure to also account for the desired level of work quality you expect from your telephone staff.

Get the telephones "off stage," separating the work of the telephones from the face-to-face visit with the patient.

During periods of low call volume, rotate new telephone staff to the clinical area to observe patient flow and "shadow" a nurse to improve knowledge and decision-making skills.

At least once a year, ask each employee: "What is the one thing that I can get for you so that you can do your job better?"

Print ribbons to hang under your nametags or small signs to adhere to your workstations that say "The First 10 Seconds." This message serves as a reminder of the importance of your initial interaction with the caller.

Sample script: "I would be happy to answer your question, and you may find other useful information on our Website at www.practicename.com."

Post answers to common questions on your practice's Website or online patient portal, thereby reducing the need for patients to call you with routine questions.

Keep writing tablets near all telephones. As soon as the caller states his or her name, write it down. Otherwise, you may forget the name as you listen to the details of the request, forcing you to ask for the caller's name again at the end of the conversation. The caller may wonder what other information you missed. After you have the name, use it as often as you can during the conversation. The name offers a connection to the patient, and demonstrates that you are listening and attentive.

Conclude every call with "Thank you for choosing our practice for your care." It demonstrates your appreciation – and acknowledges the fact that the patient made a choice.

The telephone can leave staff members with the impression that they are somehow detached from patient care. Emphasize that every *telephone call is a life. Particularly for telephone staff who are not located in the clinical area, hang pictures of patients as a reminder of the important connection that the telephone staff has with patients even when they can't see them face to face.*

You can sense someone's attitude through the telephone. Make a point of smiling as you speak – patients will sense that smile – even over the telephone.

When a caller complains, make an affirmative statement such as "Thank you for bringing that to our attention" or "I'm sorry that we didn't meet your expectations." The manager should call every patient who registers a formal complaint. Even if the complaint cannot be resolved, the acknowledgment alone proves to the patient that the practice recognizes its patients' concerns.

Documentation and appropriate management of every telephone call are vital. Emphasize to staff and providers that every telephone call represents a patient's life.

Embrace communication methods that do not require synchronous work. The use of an online patient portal, secure e-mail message, or text message shifts work to platforms that are more efficient and minimizes inbound telephone calls.

Set a goal of first-call resolution. Every message costs your practice, on average, $15.

Eliminate or dramatically reduce the use of voicemail. Voicemail is simply a method of batching and delaying the work. Instead, create real-time, one-touch strategies to respond to callers.

Establish a service promise – a turnaround time – for callbacks.

A cutoff time for callbacks is likely not sustainable in the future; 24/7 access capability is the new, expected way of doing business.

If you use voicemail, create formal policies and procedures related to its use. Voicemail should be used sparingly and should not be used to screen calls or avoid answering the telephones.

Be sure your voicemail greeting is pleasant, appropriate in tone and speed, and concise yet instructive.

Develop a goal of first-time resolution for all calls. This may require consideration of how calls are routed and to whom, but avoiding voicemail increases efficiency.

Make a simple rule: Pick up the telephone if you're not already on another call (and can't put that caller on hold to answer the other line or have it routed to an operator); use voicemail only when you're not available.

Spend time planning for your automatic call distributor. It can create the opportunity to better route, handle, and categorize calls; however, it can also backfire and frustrate callers if it is not well managed.

List no more than five options on your automated attendant; and if using sub-menus, the caller should not have to choose more than two options to reach a live person.

Patients don't get mad at automated attendants; they get mad at feeling trapped and not reaching the right person. Before going live on the system, test the technology and make sure it is working as intended.

Investigate telephony applications that integrate with your systems to place outbound calls to patients – such as appointment reminders – freeing up telephone staff for tasks that are knowledge intensive.

While patients are waiting on hold, use the opportunity to deliver custom messages about your practice, such as an invitation to register for your online patient portal.

A call center offers the opportunity to consolidate the initial contact with the practice to a group of dedicated staff with focused training. Measure the quality of the call center by its service level. Service level is the percentage of calls that are answered within a pre-defined wait threshold.

To determine if a call center will benefit your practice, evaluate the current quality of your telephones and the current staffing levels to ascertain the magnitude of improvement opportunity. Then outline the delegated authority you would want to provide to the call center staff to manage the key reasons for inbound calls. This will help you assess the need for a consolidated call center operation.

To determine the appropriate staffing model for your call center, use basic forecasting, the Erlang C method, and/or workforce management tools. The goal is to develop a staffing model aligned with both call volumes and quality expectations.

Employ part-time staff to meet service-level expectations. This permits a call center to maintain a consistent, high level of quality throughout the day at a fraction of the cost.

Establish first-call resolution as a goal and deploy strategies to make this goal a reality for your telephone operation.

Adopt best agent routing to link the caller to the staff member best qualified to meet the caller's needs. This helps the call center to have higher first-call resolution and it lowers hold times.

The most efficient state of a call center employee is for the employee to be 85 percent productive. Make sure your call center staff meets this productivity threshold.

Adopt call leveling, such as a virtual hold system, to look for opportunities to transfer work to times of predictably lower volume.

Create a knowledge center. For example, automate the scheduling logic and develop a series of questions and scripts to help call center staff link patients to the appropriate provider.

Institute patient advisors into the call center training program to share their interactions with the call center and to help staff develop empathy and other skills to improve their performance.

Framing personal stories and pictures of patients within a call center reinforces the importance of displaying empathy in every telephone interaction.

Develop a service level agreement that outlines the service expectations of the call center and the practice. Ensure that the call center meets established quality thresholds and the practice meets callback timelines.

A successful call center is an investment, not a cost. When effectively operated, a call center is an essential driver of practice profits.